CONCISE GUIDE TO
Marital and
Family Therapy

American Psychiatric Press

CONCISE GUIDES

Robert E. Hales, M.D.
Series Editor

CONTENTS

PART I
OVERVIEW OF THE FIELD OF
MARITAL AND FAMILY THERAPY

**PART II
THE PRACTICE OF
RELATIONSHIP THERAPY**

3. TEN GUIDELINES AND TECHNIQUES FOR PRACTICE . . 41

4. REDECISION RELATIONSHIP THERAPY 89

5. THE PRACTICE OF REDECISION RELATIONSHIP THERAPY 119

PART III
SPECIAL CONSIDERATIONS IN
MARITAL AND FAMILY THERAPY

6. SPECIAL POPULATIONS 153

9. CONCLUSION **227**

Index **231**

ACKNOWLEDGMENTS

We are very grateful to David Boschen, M.F.C.C., who contributed his expertise in the section on children and adolescents. We especially thank Barbara Marinacci for her expert editorial assistance—she persisted under trying circumstances—and Greg Kuny at the American Psychiatric Press, both of whom helped make this book more readable. We also appreciate the International Transactional Analysis Association for allowing us to include parts of material previously published in the *Journal of the International Transactional Analysis Association.* We also thank Jeff Zeig, Ph.D., and Brunner/Mazel, who allowed us to use some of the material previously published in *Brief Therapy: Myths, Methods and Metaphors* (Edited by Zeig J, Munion W. New York, Brunner/Mazel, 1990, pp. 135–150).

We offer very special thanks to Bob (posthumously) and Mary Goulding. They created Redecision Therapy, which is one of the cornerstones of our work, mentored us, and befriended us. Mary offered encouragement, support, and guidance throughout the process of writing this book.

ACKNOWLEDGMENTS

ABOUT THE AUTHORS

Leslie B. Kadis, M.D., a psychiatrist in private practice in the San Francisco area and Aptos, California, has been using his family therapy skills to focus on consultations to small businesses in which the family plays a critical role in the functioning of the business. He is cofounder of the Institute for Family Business, a consulting organization offering services to family firms across the United States, and is on the editorial board of the *Family Business Review,* a journal of the Family Firm Institute.

Dr. Kadis is the coauthor of a book on family therapy, *Chocolate Pudding and Other Approaches to Intensive Multiple Family Therapy* (Science and Behavior Books, 1983), and editor of a book on psychotherapy, *Redecision Therapy: Expanded Perspectives* (Western Institute for Group and Family Therapy, 1985). He has authored and coauthored numerous papers that have been published in professional publications and has been honored as a Fellow by the American Psychiatric Association for his professional and community work. He is an assistant clinical professor of psychiatry and the behavioral sciences at Stanford University and an assistant clinical professor of psychiatry at the Langley Porter Neuropsychiatric Institute, University of California Medical School in San Francisco. He is also coeditor of the International Division of the *American Journal of Family Therapy.*

Ruth McClendon, M.S.W., is a family therapist and consultant in the San Francisco and Monterey Bay areas of California. During the last 20 years, she has been training and teaching professionals throughout the United States, Europe, Canada, Japan, and Russia. Along with her husband, Leslie B. Kadis, M.D., she has developed the model for Redecision Family Therapy.

Ms. McClendon is coauthor of a book on family therapy, *Chocolate Pudding and Other Approaches to Intensive Multiple Family Therapy* (Science and Behavior Books, 1983), and has authored many articles on her work with couples and families. She has served as president of the International Transactional Analysis Association, coeditor of the International Division of the *American Journal of Family Therapy,* and on the clinical faculty at the Langley Porter Neuropsychiatric Institute, University of California Medical School in San Francisco. She is also a founding member of the Family Firm Institute and a teaching member of the American Association of Marital and Family Therapists.

INTRODUCTION

to the American Psychiatric Press Concise Guides

The American Psychiatric Press *Concise Guides* series provides practical information for psychiatrists, psychiatry residents, and medical students working in a variety of treatment settings, such as inpatient psychiatry units, outpatient clinics, consultation-liaison services, or private office settings. The *Concise Guides* are meant to complement the more detailed information to be found in lengthier psychiatry texts.

The *Concise Guides* address topics of special concern to psychiatrists in clinical practice. The books in this series contain a detailed table of contents, along with an index, tables, figures, and other charts for easy access. The books are designed to fit into a lab coat pocket or jacket pocket, which makes them a convenient source of information. The number of references has been limited to those most relevant to the material presented.

Leslie B. Kadis, M.D., and Ruth McClendon, M.S.W., are a dynamic husband-and-wife team who have collaborated in writing *Concise Guide to Marital and Family Therapy*. Dr. Kadis is a noted psychiatrist, family therapist, and business consultant. He has been a member of the editorial board of the *Family Business Review*. Ruth McClendon is a social worker and marital and family therapist. She is a past president of the International Transactional Analysis Association and past member of the board of directors of the American Group Psychotherapy Association. Together, Dr. Kadis and Ms. McClendon have coauthored another book on family therapy, *Chocolate Pudding and Other Approaches to Intensive Multiple Family Therapy*. Dr. Kadis has also edited a book on psychotherapy, *Redecision Therapy: Expanded Perspectives*.

In today's managed care environment, clinicians in all disciplines are faced with the challenge to provide brief, targeted therapy for individuals, couples, and families. *Concise Guide to Marital and Family Therapy* provides the needed information for clinicians to be able to provide effective counseling to both couples and families. The book is divided into three parts: an overview of the field of marital and family therapy; the practice of relationship therapy; and special considerations in marital and family therapy. Dr. Kadis and Ms. McClendon are the creators of the unique form of family therapy called Redecision Relationship Therapy, and clinicians should find their approach to be a very effective paradigm to use in a wide variety of situations.

Dr. Kadis and Ms. McClendon begin this concise guide, in Chapter 1, with a discussion of the basics of relationship therapy, including a definition of terms such as *family, family therapy, family systems,* and *thinking family.* The authors also provide an excellent summary concerning the indications and contraindications for this type of therapy and explain why it was developed. In Chapter 2 the authors focus on the origins of different approaches to family therapy and provide a nice synopsis of each of these different treatment approaches.

In Part II the authors describe the specific techniques of relationship therapy. Chapter 3 offers guidelines and techniques for putting relationship therapy into clinical practice. The authors provide the reader with a number of excellent tables that summarize major points in this chapter. Chapter 4 provides more detailed information on Redecision Relationship Therapy, the model that Dr. Kadis and Ms. McClendon have used so successfully in their extensive consulting work and clinical practice. In Chapter 5 the reader is provided with two examples—one involving a couple and the other, a family—in which relationship therapy was applied.

In Part III Dr. Kadis and Ms. McClendon begin with a discussion of the application of relationship therapy to marital and sex therapy. They then discuss the application of relationship therapy to special populations: gay and lesbian couples and their families, children and adolescents, reconstituted families, families with substance abuse, families with chronic illness, and families with elderly members. Clinicians reading this chapter will find the authors' discussion especially valuable in applying relationship therapy to work with each of these populations. For those interested in group therapy, Chapter 7 gives more detailed information on how relationship therapy may be applied to group therapy with couples and families and in consultation to family-owned businesses. The authors end the book by discussing ethical considerations in relationship therapy, addressing topics such as determining who is the patient, confidentiality, therapeutic neutrality, and dealing with managed care.

As someone with limited skills in working with couples, families, and groups, I found *Concise Guide to Marital and Family Therapy* to be extremely practical and filled with sound clinical pearls. The authors include a number of helpful tables and figures throughout their book that summarize and highlight important concepts. Their writing style is such that readers will find themselves feeling as if they were in a teaching session with the authors. What also comes through in this book is that the authors are excellent clinicians with a wealth of information that they have gained from their busy practices and have included in their book. Consequently, the reader may rest assured that this is not simply a theoretical approach, but one that has been very successful in clinical practice.

Concise Guide to Marital and Family Therapy is invaluable reading for psychiatry residents and psychiatrists, psychologists, social workers, and marital and family therapists. The principles and techniques that Les Kadis and Ruth McClendon discuss in their book are invaluable for anyone practicing this form of therapy. Their model, Redecision Relationship Therapy, is one that makes a great deal of sense and is easily applicable to a variety of clinical settings. *Concise Guide to Marital and Family Therapy* is a wonderful addition to the concise guide series published by the American Psychiatric Press, and the authors are congratulated for a job well done.

PREFACE

We live in a complex world, a world of numerous reciprocal relationships. Most of us interact daily with our partners, children, colleagues, and neighbors, as well as with numerous people who provide the services for living life. All of these interactions have an impact on us, and we in turn have an impact on them. When they support a positive view of ourselves, we feel at peace; when they don't, we feel anxious.

The individual approach in therapy is one of helping people manage the anxiety derived from the difficult interactions of daily life by focusing on the internalized components of those interactions as revealed by each patient. Another approach in therapy is to focus on the relationships between the people themselves. Each approach has its advantages and disadvantages. Each has its place.

In this book we focus on therapy with families and couples—nowadays encompassed by the field of marital and family therapy (MFT). This book is about changing relationships through changing the interactions among the people who make up the family or marital unit. It is also important to note that the ideas we discuss are frequently applied outside the MFT setting. For instance, consultants use the principles and techniques presented here in both corporate and family business environments. Attorneys use the ideas and techniques of relationship therapy to facilitate arbitration, and social scientists draw on the theories of family therapy to better understand the complex web of entire cultures. Despite the setting, these therapists, consultants, facilitators, and scholarly observers of society are *thinking family,* or, in other words, thinking about the family as a system—they have in mind the complex web of relationships, the pattern of transactions that repeat themselves, and the unspoken rules that drive these transactions, regardless of which aspect of the family they are addressing.

In Part I of this concise guide we present an integrated view of the field of MFT, or relationship therapy. We first consider the meanings and implications of certain terms, such as family systems, and suggest which patient situations are most or least suitable for relationship therapy. We then take a brief look at the history of MFT and summarize the relevant schools of therapies, theories, and resultant main approaches to relationship treatment.

In Part II we describe the practice of MFT, or relationship therapy, first focusing on the relationship therapist's practice orientation, and then moving through the various stages of treatment to conclusion. The "tools of the trade" and their essential features—including how to use them in situations ranging from assessment to devising and then implementing a treatment plan—are presented within the context of 10 basic guidelines to successful therapy. Then, to exemplify how these guidelines and tools can be utilized within a particular framework for practice, we describe the approach we customarily use in our own practices, separately and together, Redecision Relationship Therapy (RRT). Drawing on and integrating aspects of several theoretical approaches, this model offers a structure that provides a home for most psychotherapeutic orientations. To show how RRT "works" in helping couples, families, and other relationships to heal, we tell in some depth the stories of a family and a couple as they progress through the three distinctive stages of the model.

In Part III we take up different applications of relationship therapy that have proven particularly effective and useful: with special populations (such as families with chronically ill, elderly persons, gay and lesbian partners, children and adolescents, and members who are substance abusers); with couples or multiple-family groups; and with family members involved in family-owned or -controlled businesses, when the role of relationship therapist changes to that of relationship consultant. Finally, we look at some of the ethical considerations related to complex issues that are likely to come up during the course of relationship therapy.

Our goal in this book is to present both the theoretical and the practical cornerstones of relationship therapy that help therapists move a family or couple toward healing. As Mary Pipher says so eloquently in *The Shelter of Each Other,*

> Therapists have enormous power to do good or ill in families. We are called upon to explain behavior and to say something is happening. When a delinquent adolescent boy comes in, we can ask about his parents' relationship, his friends, the music he listens to or the school he attends. When a woman comes in depressed, we can ask questions about her exercise, diet and use of chemicals, her health, her marriage, her work or her childhood. Our questions suggest causes and lead clients toward solutions. We can ask questions that pull for pathology or questions that bring out strengths. We can ask questions that increase distancing and scapegoating of family members. Or we can ask questions that begin the healing. (1)

■ REFERENCE

Pipher M: The Shelter of Each Other: Rebuilding Our Families. New York, Putnam, 1996, p 27

PART I

OVERVIEW OF THE FIELD OF MARITAL AND FAMILY THERAPY

THE BASICS

Definitions are important. Too often, particularly in the context of relationships, we think we agree about the meaning of our words, only to find later that we were wrong. This is particularly likely to happen when the concepts apply to universal experiences, which, in spite of their universality, are highly individual. It is important to look behind the definitions to the concepts that are embedded in them. This will ensure that we are all on the same train. So let's look now at the basic concepts behind some of the terms we use: What is meant today when therapists refer to "the family," "family therapy," "family systems," and to the concept "thinking family"?

■ DEFINING TERMS

Throughout this book you will find the terms *marital therapy, couple* (or *couples*) *therapy, marital and family therapy* (MFT), and *relationship therapy*. We use all these terms and apologize for any confusion. "Marital and family therapy" is used in the title of this concise guide because that is the historically correct term. But since "marital" refers to the legal status of the couple, and since the dominant paradigm is the *system,* we prefer the term relationship therapy. The same is true for the family component of MFT in that the dominant paradigm is also the system. Relationship therapy is a term that reflects the nature and primary object of the therapeutic work, applies equally to the couple and the family components, and reflects the fact that the relationship is common to both a couple and a family. The key definitions used in this book are summarized in Table 1–1.

Family

(Defining "family" presents some difficulty, because in the modern-day world each of us has a different concept of family. Our unique understanding of family is born out of current experiences with our nuclear families as well as our history with our family of origin. Both the past and the present experience are tempered by contemporary sociocultural realities.)

As we approach the end of the 20th century, fewer than 51% of American children living today will grow up in the traditional two-parent, "nuclear" family. For the other 49% of children, other ways of child-rearing have become the norm: single-parent families, step, or "blended," families, adoptive families, grandparents-as-guardians families, foster families, families with same-sex parents, and even group homes. Furthermore, the ever-increasing prevalence of working mothers has led to major change within the traditional American family. In fact, sociologists point out that the very idea of a traditional family with a stay-at-home wife and mother is becoming an unattainable ideal. This seemingly radical

TABLE 1–1.	**Key definitions in marital and family (relationship) therapy**
Relationship therapy	Any form of psychotherapeutic endeavor that focuses on altering interpersonal interactions
Family, marital, or couples therapy	Relationship therapy with a specific relationship unit
Family	Any group that defines itself as a family
Relationship systems	A way of conceptualizing relationships in which the focus is on the functioning of the unit as a whole rather than the individual parts
Thinking family	Keeping the entire current family system in mind regardless of who is in the room

position is supported by evidence such as the observation that "more than three-fifths of married women with dependent children are in the labor force, as well as a majority of mothers of infants, while there are more than twice as many single-mother families as married, homemaker-mom families" (1, p. 6). The trends in most of the Western world are comparable.

Given this diversity of both form and function, it is difficult to derive a definition of family. Many who write about family therapy consider the family to be a group of people who have a kinship bond and currently share a common experience. Although still too narrow to take in the full range of family configurations that cross the threshold of family therapists, this definition is useful because it distinguishes the family from other affinity groups. Members of work groups, for example—except for family-owned businesses—share a current experience and may have a long history together, but they rarely share a kinship bond. Similarly, friendship groups, as well as groups that come together under various auspices such as a common religious affiliation, meet some but not all of the requirements.

We have chosen to beg this question of defining family and to permit our own intuition to guide us. If a group of people think of themselves as a family, then, as family therapists interested in the nature of the relationships, we consider this an appropriate unit to investigate.

Family Therapy

It is equally difficult to define family therapy. The generally accepted definition is "any psychotherapeutic endeavor that explicitly focuses on altering the interaction between or among family members and seeks to improve the functioning of the family as a unit, or its subsystems and/or the functioning of individual members of the family" (2, p. 565). We accept and follow this definition with one caveat: It is not necessary to meet with the entire family in order to alter or improve the functioning of the family unit. This dictum will become apparent when we amplify the concept of thinking family.

Family Systems

The idea that the family—any and every family—operates as a system is the defining concept for MFT. A systems approach, not the number of people in the room, is what differentiates MFT from individual therapy. It is, however, difficult to obtain a working understanding of systems because the Western world is linear—we think in terms of beginnings and endings, cause and effect. Systems, however, are anything but linear.

Conceptually, a system is something—in fact, anything—made up of interacting parts. Thus, we can talk about a machine as a system, a government as a system, a single-cell organism as a system, or a group of people as a system (3). When any particular system is discussed, it is described from the perspective of the way the various parts interact rather than of the individual parts themselves. Although a car engine contains cylinders and pistons and many other parts, we think of it as a car engine and describe it from the perspective of how all the parts interact to enable the engine to work.

Systems theorists recognize that a car engine is very different from what one might expect just from seeing the components laid out on a table. A therapist looks at a family system in an analogous way. Any family is different from what might be inferred from knowing the individual persons who make up the family. The family has its own structure, its own rules, and a unique memory of the history of how it has managed through the ups and downs of life.

One way of describing a system is to describe the style or pattern of interactions. By focusing on the pattern of interactions, MFT has made its most important contribution to psychotherapy. It has changed the nature of the dialogue between patient and therapist from a focus on the *intrapsychic content*—that is, what patients are telling us—to a focus on the *interpersonal process*—that is, how family members interact with each other. This emphasis on the interpersonal process is similar to attending primarily to group process rather than to the dynamics within individuals in the group.

Unfortunately, though, it is extremely difficult to describe this shift in emphasis because we do not have adequate language. For instance, let's go back to the expulsion of Adam and Eve from the Garden of Eden; an archetypal story in Western civilization, it exemplifies our customary thinking in terms of cause and effect. Eve gave Adam the apple, Adam ate the apple, and they were both expelled from the Garden—a simple, unidirectional chain of events. In contrast, a systems approach requires us to shift from cause-and-effect to circular thinking (4). From a circular perspective, Adam and Eve are partners in a reciprocal relationship—Eve's giving of the apple depends on Adam's taking it, just as Adam could not take it if Eve did not give it—a circular chain.

In systems terms, A does not cause B; instead, A and B reciprocally interact and impact each other. Intuitively, we know this to be true because we have all heard the typical couple dialogue: A: "I wouldn't yell if he listened to me," followed by B: "I can't listen when she yells." Individual therapists for each of these people would be drawn to one or the other side of the argument, depending on how the problem was presented to them. In the systems perspective, the sequence is thought of as a circular process in which A and B react to each other. There is no beginning and no end.

One important corollary of the idea of circular causality is that our description of the problem—how we talk about it and how we intervene—depends on how we punctuate the A-causes-B-causes-A sequence. Systems therapists are ever aware that their personal viewpoint introduces an important variable into understanding the relationship (5).

Within this oversimplified version of a typical interpersonal dilemma, the task of the systems therapist is to describe the sequence of interactions in such a way that an appropriate intervention can result in positive change. There are several ways the therapist can do this, and, as we discuss below, the differences are more of style, or therapist/theorist preference, than of substance. Using the A-and-B example above, the systems theorist could describe the recursive nature of those specific transactions (and of others like them that would invariably be discovered) and use a term such as "symmetrical relationship" to note that each statement is matched by a subsequent statement, so that there is continuous escalation. The expanding, intensifying, ongoing fight between a couple or between siblings is typical of a symmetrical relationship.

One characteristic of the systems approach is that descriptions do not suggest cause. They do, however, allow different possibilities to intervene. A classic systems intervention is to prescribe fighting, but in a ritualized manner. In this way an uncontrolled experience is brought under control without the therapist's ever having to enter the argument. A different systems therapist, working with the same couple, might attend to the structure of the relationship.

A therapist interested in relationship structure (6) might observe that the partners finish each other's statements—possibly an indication that interpersonal boundaries are unclear. In this case the therapist could introduce exercises during sessions and suggest homework that will promote differentiation. Alternatively, the therapist might notice that neither of the partners listens to the other—an indication that boundaries are too rigid. The therapist might then help the couple soften those boundaries under the protection of traditional communication training.

Finally, it is possible to decipher the hidden rules that govern the operations of the recursive patterns and then to conclude that this couple acts as if they believe "You have to yell to be heard," or "No one listens," or perhaps "It's not okay to talk about hurts." The relationship therapist might address these hidden belief systems directly by using a historical approach, or indirectly by using a behavioral approach that reinforces and rewards listening. Whichever approach the relationship therapist chooses, he or she will be adopting a broader perspective than that provided by just listening to the content, heeding the intrapsychic conflicts, and attending to the defenses.

Thinking Family

Lastly, we want to define how the important concept of *thinking family* applies to treatment. Earlier, the prevailing belief in the field of family counseling required a marital and family therapist to include the entire relationship unit in the office in order to evaluate the system and design the appropriate intervention. It is still important to meet with the entire family to understand how the system works. However, we now know that it is not necessary to meet with everyone to effect change in the family's pattern of interaction. We have learned to respect the power of one individual to impact the entire family unit. Making the most of this power requires thinking family: keeping the entire current family system in mind regardless of who is in our office.

Understanding the reciprocal interactions between the family as a system and the individual has led to a broadening of the focus for interventions in relationship therapy to include the individual. If we keep the systems perspective in mind, even when we are working with just one patient, we will be thinking family and doing relationship therapy.

This widening of the focus of MFT to also include the individual while thinking family is both historically and conceptually significant. Early in the history of the field, interventions were designed mainly to change the interactional pattern, because the pattern itself was believed to be the source of the problem. Although this belief continues to be true to some extent today, modern-day practitioners, as mentioned, include interventions targeted toward specific individuals in the family unit as well.

Some theorists, wanting to separate the individual from what has been called the "undifferentiated ego mass" (7), focus on the individual, keeping one eye on the family system. Others in the field do this from a strategic standpoint, holding to the view that if one individual changes, the interactional pattern of the family will change. These two viewpoints have led to the development of schools of thinking that believe it is possible to conduct marital therapy when only one partner is present (8).

The essential point is that MFT refers to a way of conceptualizing a therapeutic framework as much as it refers to a specific therapeutic modality or school of therapy. In other words, even though many family therapists do not meet with the family as a whole, the ideas and approaches of family therapy are paramount in their approaches because they "think family."

This idea of *thinking family* is particularly useful for individually oriented psychotherapists because it opens the door to different ways of conceptualizing the mental models of patients. Thinking family involves adopting a broader perspective with whomever is in the office and thereby using a systems approach to impact the entire social unit.

■ INDICATIONS AND CONTRAINDICATIONS

As with any new field, relationship therapy was first thought of as a panacea for what ails the patient. It took hold partly in reaction to the long-term psychoanalytic approach that had been the dominant paradigm for psychotherapy in the preceding years, and partly because the emerging data describing seriously disturbed communications in the families of schizophrenic patients (9) pointed away from intrapsychic causality.

These data led to one popular early formulation: the idea of the "schizophrenogenic mother." Hence, it is not surprising that at that time the family was often considered the root of individual problems and that, therefore, family therapy was indicated. However, over time, with more thorough research and a better understanding of biologic factors and their interaction with psychosocial factors, it became clearer when and when not to prescribe some form of relationship therapy.

Today, outcome research provides some criteria for prescribing relationship therapy. Based on meta-analysis, either marital or family therapy is specifically indicated to facilitate the treatment of a severely mentally ill family member, whether to foster compliance with medication, mobilize resources, minimize the likelihood of rehospitalization, or ameliorate stress in the caregivers (10). In other, similar studies, therapy aimed at improving the couple relationship is also specifically indicated when one of the members is depressed or when a conduct disorder or substance abuse is present in the family (11).

An important indication for initiating one or more relationship interviews—a relative indication—is the presence of a psychophysiologic disorder. Some of the earliest research in the field of family therapy demonstrated that the condition of juvenile diabetics was more stable after family therapy and that anorexic patients gained and maintained their weight when family therapy was part of the therapeutic strategy (12).

Overall, there is usually good cause for a therapist to test the waters for relationship therapy by meeting for at least one conjoint session with the partner or the entire family of any primary patient. The general indications and contraindications for relationship therapy are summarized in Table 1–2.

■ RATIONALE FOR RELATIONSHIP THERAPY

We all live in relationships. It's just a fact. As people, rich or poor, male or female, young or old, we all have relationships that are important to us. No one starts afresh every morning, for even the isolated have people they have met before in their lives and people they will meet in the future.

Some relationships work better than others. Some will last a lifetime, and others will finish early, some even before they leave the starting gate. Tolstoy's famous comment that happy families are all alike and unhappy families are all unhappy in their own way is not true. Each family is unique because each relationship is unique.

When relationships fail, people become unhappy, and they often become symptomatic. Conversely, when external events intervene, the stress often has an adverse impact on the relationship and taxes the family's ability to cope with the event. We discussed this reciprocal interaction earlier in this chapter. Fortunately, there is some good news.

TABLE 1–2.	Indications and contraindications for relationship therapy

Relationship therapy is **indicated**

When there is a crisis or major life transition in the relationship

When the onset of symptoms is connected to relationship disharmony

When the patient is a child or adolescent, and there are either health, educational, or legal problems

As an adjunct to medical treatment or psychotherapy—to gather or impart information

Relationship therapy is **contraindicated**

When the therapeutic environment is not safe and someone will be harmed by information, uncontrolled anxiety, or hostility

When there is a lack of willingness to be honest

When there is an unwillingness to maintain confidentiality

Recently, the *Journal of Marital and Family Therapy* devoted an entire issue to a review of the outcome research for the field. Shadish and colleagues (13, p. 345), in the opening to their article, sum up the field: "Family therapy works . . . at least as well as other forms of psychotherapy . . ." Moreover, families entering relationship therapy have a 65% chance of feeling better as a result of the experience (14). This is a very good result for any therapeutic endeavor, and it is very good news.

Finally, it is important to note that the results of failures to solve relationship difficulties can be disastrous; divorce, domestic violence, decreased economic status, and an interruption in the pursuit of life goals are only a few of the possible consequences. It is essential that we do whatever we can to mitigate this distress.

■ REFERENCES

1. Stacey J: In the Name of the Family: Rethinking Family Values in the Postmodern Age. Boston, MA, Beacon Press, 1996
2. Gurman AS, Kniskern DP, Pinsof W: Research on the process and outcome of family therapy, in Handbook of Psychotherapy and Behav-

ior Change, 3rd Edition. Edited by Garfield SL, Bergin AE. New York, Wiley, 1986, pp 565–624

3. Miller J: Toward a general theory for the behavioral sciences. Am Psychol 10:695–704, 1955

4. Selvini-Palazzoli M, Boscolo L, Cecchin G, et al: Paradox and Counterparadox: A New Model for Therapy in the Family in Schizophrenic Transition. New York, Jason Aronson, 1978

5. Watzlawick P, Weakland JH, Fisch R. Change: Principles of Problem Formation and Problem Resolution. New York, WW Norton, 1974

6. Minuchin S, Montalvo B, Guerney B, et al: Families of the Slums: An Exploration of Their Structure and Treatment. New York, Basic Books, 1967

7. Bowen M: Family Therapy in Clinical Practice. Northvale, NJ, Jason Aronson, 1978

8. Wiener-Davis M: Divorce Busting. New York, Fireside, 1992

9. Wynne LC, Singer MT: Pseudo-mutuality in the family relations of schizophrenics. Arch Gen Psychiatry 9:161–206, 1963

10. Pinsof W, Wynne LC: The efficacy of marital and family therapy: overview and conclusions. Journal of Marital and Family Therapy 21:585–616. 1995

11. Prince S, Jacobson N: A review and evaluation of marital and family therapy for affective disorders. Journal of Marital and Family Therapy 21:377–402, 1995

12. Minuchin S, Rosman B, Baker L: Psychosomatic Families: Anorexia Nervosa in Context. Cambridge, MA, Harvard University Press, 1978

13. Shadish W, Ragsdale K, Glasser R, et al: The efficacy and effectiveness of marital and family therapy: a perspective from meta-analysis. Journal of Marital and Family Therapy 21:345–360, 1995

14. Shadish W, Montgomery L, Wilson P, et al: The effects of family and marital psychotherapies: a meta-analysis. J Consult Clin Psychol 61:992–1002, 1993

2

THE DEVELOPMENT OF DIFFERENT APPROACHES

New paradigms rarely emerge fully developed; they result from new ideas being added to a foundation built of older ideas. Successful additions to old buildings are ones that thoughtfully integrate the best of the old with the best of the new. The new building stands on its own merits, yet we have a different appreciation of the new structure when we know its history. Following the building analogy, current models of relationship therapy are the result of adding and integrating various components from different schools to form the new model, and understanding this scholastic history is the foundation for understanding contemporary relationship therapy.

■ THE HISTORICAL PERSPECTIVE

The history of the field of marital and family therapy (MFT) is itself a metaphor for the complexity and descriptive ambiguity of the field. Although the actual time line for the development of the field is short (i.e., from the early 1950s to the present), the number of different ideas is large, and the creativity within the field is exciting.

Although family therapy and marital therapy today have enough in common to be considered one topic, historically they developed along completely separate lines and within wholly different time frames. Family therapy, by comparison, is a relative newcomer, having entered the scene in the 1950s. This fascinating history is the subject of an excellent review by Broderick and Schrader (1). The origins of marital therapy are much older than the origins of family therapy; they can be traced back to biblical times in the form of guidelines for conducting oneself with a partner. Marital therapy began as marriage counseling, originally taking the form of advice giving and counseling (most often pastoral counseling). Later, peer counseling, marriage enhancement, sex therapy, coaching, family life education, and psychoeducation became part of the marriage counseling scene. It was not until 1970, almost 10 years after family therapy had developed under the umbrella of the formal medical establishment, that marital therapy acquired a separate identity and the name was changed from marriage counseling.

The impetus for development of the field of family therapy, as distinct from marital therapy, was driven by its founders' clinical experiences. In the mid-1950s, two separate areas of investigation sprang up. In one area, a few dynamically trained therapists were beginning to meet with the families of their individual patients. In these meetings they frequently found discrepancies between what their patients were telling them and their own observations. In addition, events, perceptions, and recollections were often not what they appeared to be, and their explanatory models did not account for these discrepancies.

Concurrently, in another area, other clinicians were gathering experience with hospitalized patients, particularly those with schizophrenia. They noted that patients frequently relapsed shortly after their return home—pointing to some important negative influence exerted within the family (2). Many years later the first research-based explanations of this phenomenon were proposed, and in 1985 it was discovered that the highest relapse rates for patients with schizophrenia occurred in families that were simultaneously close and covertly hostile and critical (3). This variable, labeled "expressed emotion" (EE), has provided an important tool used in evaluating the importance of familial factors in triggering the onset of mental illness. One could almost say that the field of MFT was the result of the observations from these two areas of investigation.

■ DIFFERING PERCEPTIONS

In the fable about the blind men and the elephant, each of the four men experienced only one part of the elephant; as a result, they created four different impressions of the whole creature, based on whatever part of it each had touched. In the case of relationships, the phenomenon is different. Each person present might experience an identical event, but each individual experiences it through his or her own personal lens. In a marriage or a family, even when the experience is similarly described by the participants, the meaning attributed to the events can be decidedly different. To add to the complexity, an outside observer, such as a therapist, will likely attribute a still different meaning to the events.

The early family therapists sought to understand and explain this uniqueness of perception. Their quests fostered the many different schools of MFT that proliferated in the early days of the field and continue in the present. Exploring the interpersonal world of the patient was not such a new idea, of course; the important factor is that relationship therapists began to realize that what their patients told them was only one possible view.

In the early days of MFT, it was thought that the source of all pathology resided in the malfunctioning system (4). Some of the most elegant early research correlated specific family patterns with individual perceptions (5). Since then, that thinking has been modified to leave us with a more balanced view, in which there is recognition that both individual and relationship factors are important and that these factors affect each other.

Part of this change in direction occurred because research made it abundantly clear that individual pathology can develop in healthy as well as malfunctioning relationships. Another part of the directional change evolved in response to the gap between research and practice, which resulted in the inability to carry out clinically some of the basic tenets of the pure systems theorists.

A final important contributor to the change in direction came in response to the new feminist-informed theory. We learned about the importance of power, and the potential for the abuse of that power, within the family. We also were reminded that sometimes people do bad things, and began realizing that it is not always possible, safe, or even useful to maintain the strict therapeutic neutrality espoused by the pure systems therapists (6–9).

Throughout the development of the field of relationship therapy, there has been constancy in the idea that each of us exists in the context of a larger system and that our behavior affects that system and the system reciprocally affects each of us (10). Typically, the most important system is our current family—be it the marital dyad, our immediate or extended family, our family of origin, or the mental model of a family that we carry with us wherever we go.

It follows, then, that any mental health professional who seeks to help the individual patient is best served if he or she understands the family system of the patient and uses the tool of *thinking family* (see Chapter 1).

■ CURRENT STATE OF THE FIELD

One day, while we were trying to learn the finer points of tennis, our instructor pointed out that there are countless ways of holding the racquet, different styles for the backstroke and the follow-through, and multiple possibilities for the way a player stands. Professional tennis players demonstrate and win with many of them. He then went on to remind us that when it comes time to hit the ball, regardless of the style, the laws of physics take over—and the ball goes where the racquet face sends it.

The many different approaches to MFT are something like the tennis stroke. Treatment possibilities have become too numerous to count, even though there are fewer than the reputed 400 different approaches to psychotherapy in general. All the while, relationship therapists are always working to further understand and organize the "laws of physics" as they apply to helping marital and family relationships change in positive ways.

Fortunately, outcome research points the way to a system that organizes the different approaches of MFT through a combination of theory and commonality of approach. According to the research, there are two basic forms of MFT (Table 2–1): *insight-oriented marital and family therapy* and *behavioral marital and family therapy* (11). Surprisingly, virtually all the theoretical approaches or schools can be classified in one of these two ways. A few integrative approaches successfully combine elements of both insight-oriented and behavioral approaches, and since these tend to be more practical than theoretical, they will be addressed separately.

■ INSIGHT-ORIENTED MARITAL AND FAMILY THERAPY

The insight-oriented approaches to MFT (also known as the growth-oriented or developmentally oriented approaches) (Table 2–2) have their roots firmly planted in psychoanalytic theory. Although they do not necessarily use the psychoanalytic method, they do target their work toward understanding (12). Typically, the insight-oriented approaches can be used first to locate the important affect, then to trace the roots of the affect to the early experience, and finally to understand and explain the current conflict in the context of that early experience.

TABLE 2–1.   **Approaches to relationship therapy**

Approach	Underlying beliefs
Insight-oriented	Affect leads to insight Insight leads to transformation
Behavioral	Behavioral change leads to attitudinal change Attitudinal change leads to emotional change
Integrative	Integration accommodates relationship, individual, and therapist variables

The methods for uncovering affect and developing insight are specific to each approach, but when it comes to "hitting the ball," the "laws of physics take over." Within an insight-oriented approach to relationship therapy, family members or marital partners gain a new understanding of the person who is the current focus. In addition, the person who is the focus is, in accordance with the ideas of MFT, affected by the attitudinal and, possibly, behavioral changes of other family members.

TABLE 2–2. **Insight-oriented marital and family therapy approaches**

Approach	Founder(s)	Therapeutic focus
Psychodynamic	Ackerman	Understanding defensive patterns and the transferential nature of relationships
Object relations	Scharff and Scharff	Interpretation of projection and projective identification
Family of origin	Bowen	Facilitation of separation and individuation from family of origin
Contextual	Boszormenyi-Nagy	Ethical perspectives on the multiplicity of obligations and responsibilities people have toward each other
Postmodern	White	Interpersonal conflict as resulting from differing realities Construction of new stories, leading to healing
Experiential	Satir/Whitaker	Insight gained through experience

Here are brief sketches of the six major insight-oriented approaches.

Psychodynamic Therapy

The psychodynamic relationship therapy model is probably the most familiar of the insight-oriented approaches (13). Affect leads to insight, and insight leads to transformation. The main foci are understanding the defensive patterns of the family and each of its individual members and understanding the transferential nature of relationships between the family members as well as with the therapist.

The primary techniques used by relationship therapists here draw on the techniques of both psychodynamic individual and group therapy: building the therapeutic alliance over time, working toward insight and interpretation, encouraging free association, and allowing the transference to develop.

It is not too much of a stretch to recognize transference as a here-and-now phenomenon and, by extension, to recognize that families will go to great lengths to stabilize their relationships by avoiding change. *Transference to the group* is a generally accepted prerequisite for successful group therapy. Its manifestation in family life as *cohesiveness* is simply another form of the transference phenomenon. Since cohesiveness is perhaps the single most consistent factor that defines the healthy family, the development of cohesiveness is an important therapeutic goal. In psychodynamically oriented family therapy, this occurs when people reveal their innermost thoughts, dreams, and fantasies and are able to explore unconscious material. Psychodynamically oriented relationship therapists encourage free association by structuring the environment to make it safe for family members to say anything and everything. They then confront the resistance to open communication.

In the earliest forms of psychodynamic family therapy, therapists interviewed a family member while other members of the family were present, and then explored the family members' reactions, again from a psychodynamic perspective. A variation of this technique, called the "fish bowl," has become an important component used by some relationship therapists who work with multiple-family groups (14) or other affinity groups in different settings. It has also become part of the reflecting team approach, in which members of the team of therapists sit behind a one-way mirror until some crucial point in the proceedings, when they enter the consultation room and report their observations to the family and the in-room therapists.

Relationship therapists differ in both style and focus in their use of the psychodynamic approach. Paul and Paul (15) focus on the unresolved grieving process, Stierlin (16) addresses the adolescent struggle for independence, and Framo (17) focuses on the spousal or familial reenactment of conflicts that existed in the family of origin. For marital therapy, Bader and Pearson (18), using a model rooted in developmental theory, aim to facilitate individuation in the couple. Irrespective of whether the focus is the couple or the family, the goal of psychodynamically oriented relationship therapists is to uncover the affect, track it to the early belief, expose the belief, and create a new understanding.

Object Relations Therapy

The object relations approach is probably the most prevalent of the psychodynamically oriented forms of relationship therapy, possibly because of the thoughtful writings of its main proponents, Scharff and Scharff (19). Object relations family therapists emphasize the importance of projection and projective identification in maintaining the distortions that confound marital and family interactions (19, 20). They theorize that because the objects, as defined by the theory, are simultaneously real and unconscious, projection and projective identification occur in real time in the relationship therapist's office. In this approach, projective identification is addressed directly through interpretation, with the basic tenet common to the insight-oriented therapies maintained: that insight and understanding lead to transformation.

Family-of-Origin Therapy

Using a developmental or intergenerational paradigm, Murray Bowen focused on the issues of separation and individuation (21). In this formulation, the primary task of the individual is to separate and individuate from the "undifferentiated ego mass" of his or her family of origin. Failure to do so results in the failure to acquire clear self boundaries, which is associated with anxiety and impacts the entire family unit.

Understanding Bowen's approach depends on understanding the nature and impact of transgenerational patterns and bonds. Bowen's ideas of a family emotional system, of multigenerational transmission of symptoms, beliefs, and attitudes, and of triangulation have become part of the thinking of most contemporary family therapists (22).

The latter concept, *triangulation,* is now a standard part of the general psychotherapeutic lexicon because it serves many purposes. It refers to a process in which two people in conflict reduce the tension by incorporating a third person into the relationship. For example, when a couple is in open conflict, one partner may develop a special relationship with one of the children in order to defuse the conflict.

In addition to managing open conflict, triangulation can be brought into play when one or both partners have difficulties with closeness or distance. This dynamic is commonly present when there is an extramarital affair. The third person can meet the need for closeness in one person and/or divert the anxiety over closeness in the other. Triangles can be used in this way to help manage both internal and interpersonal stress. Partners thereby provide structure for each other and in doing so help to reduce anxiety. When one person is unavailable for whatever reason, the third person in the triangle can fill the need for structure and reduce the intrapsychic tension.

One tool for managing triangulation is the *genogram,* one of the most important techniques of relationship therapy (23) (see discussion of Guideline 7 in Chapter 3). This instrument was developed directly from Bowen's belief in the need for individuals to separate from their family of origin. The genogram puts the entire family of origin in both historical and emotional perspective.

Bowen, one of the founders of the field of MFT, was among the first to promote the idea that a therapist can conduct a course of family therapy without working with the entire family unit. This is done by metaphorically bringing the family of origin into the therapy room. Bowen also taught us that whenever we think about the different triangles, we are, in effect, thinking about the family as a system—in other words, we are *thinking family.*

Contextual Therapy

Recognizing the interrelatedness of the individual and his or her relationships, Boszormenyi-Nagy and his colleagues (24) explored a new paradigm in which the therapeutic contract is thought of as multilateral. Contextual therapy recognizes that family members interact as individuals with the entire family as a system as well as with each other individually, while the family also functions as a unit. Multilateral contracts are formed that honor the multiplicity of obligations and responsibilities that follow from this arrangement. This concept, known as "multidirected partiality," stands as an interesting alternative to therapeutic neutrality.

Contextual therapy is a variation on the developmental theme and focuses on similar family systems issues, as do the other insight-oriented therapies; but it does so from the ethical perspective of the obligations and responsibilities that various members of the family have to each other. In contextual therapy, attention is directed to the bargains people make to get their needs met. When the family system is addressed from the perspective of reciprocal bargains, there is an implicit quid pro quo that becomes the focus of attention. This form of relationship therapy is unique among the insight-oriented approaches in that contextual therapy also incorporates a large component of education along with insight.

Postmodern Therapies

Another way of thinking about insight is from the perspective of the stories we tell ourselves about ourselves, about our history, and about our world. As children we all made up stories. We made up stories about who we were, where we came from, how we fit, first, into our family and, later, into the world; stories about loss and death; stories about order and chaos. These stories serve to orient us, guide us, and sustain us because they help us explain the events in our world. They help us make sense of the unexpected and establish predictability.

The postmodern therapies, which include constructivist and narrative therapy, were developed to account for individual stories as well as the observation that since each individual's perceptions are unique, in essence each person constructs his or her own reality (25–27). In this formulation interpersonal conflict is a consequence of differing realities bumping against each other. In the postmodern approach the common factor is, again, insight, although the understanding required is about the stories rather than the defenses or projections.

The postmodern therapist thinks of himself or herself as a "co-creator" and believes that the therapeutic element is the active structuring of questions. The questions themselves are thought to be the main therapeutic intervention. In an effort to elucidate the underlying story, a postmodern therapist might say to a man who has abused his wife, "So you think it is all right to yell at your wife when you are upset? . . . Where in your family did you learn that?"

The postmodern therapies return the focus of family therapy to one of the original concepts: that everybody in a family sees things differently. These differences create communication deviancies that ultimately lead to the development of symptoms. Since each of us constructs our own reality, the goal of postmodern relationship therapy becomes the creation of a new story (or narrative) for the family. In this way the postmodern therapies are able to deal with the turbulence and violence that plague the contemporary family because they consider how each person views the world and address those views individually.

Experiential Therapy

At first glance, the experiential approaches appear different from the other forms of insight-oriented MFT because the insight component is not as obvious. They are, however, the same as the other forms of insight-oriented MFT. Experiential approaches use affect as the guide to the early experiences in order to develop insights into the current conflict and into the self. The difference is that insight is gained on the experiential rather than the cognitive level. The work of Virginia Satir (28) and that of Carl Whitaker (29) stand out as the most prominent examples of this subgroup of insight-oriented MFT.

Satir strongly believed that the way each family member originally experienced the family environment created defensive attitudes and feelings of shame. These entrenched experiences and feelings ultimately lead to the presenting problem or problems. Her goal was to help the couple or family create and maintain new experiences that would be significantly different from the ones they had when left to their own devices. To this end, her genius lay in developing a multiplicity of techniques that touched all the senses and evoked emotions, which she then helped the family to handle in a productive way.

Many of the techniques Satir devised depend to a large extent on the effective communication of feelings and thoughts. These communication techniques are a major part of the armamentarium of most modern-day relationship therapists. Her work also stands out because it is accessible; patients intuitively understand and can easily translate her ideas into their own frame of reference.

Like Virginia Satir, Carl Whitaker made a uniquely important contribution to the field of experiential therapy. His work was different from hers in that his style was extremely personal. He depended on the force of his personality, the uniqueness of his vision, and the courage to do and say the unthinkable in the family setting. He had the ability to shake up the family in such a way that it became difficult for them to ever operate as they had before. The new experiences created for the family led, as in Satir's approach, to intuitive understandings and lasting change.

■ BEHAVIORAL MARITAL AND FAMILY THERAPY

Whereas the insight-oriented family therapist holds to the view that change occurs through understanding—or, in other words, emotional change precedes behavioral change—the behaviorally oriented marital and family therapist takes the opposite view. Behaviorally oriented therapists believe that change in behavior promotes change in attitudes and that emotional change follows behavioral change.

The work of a large group of therapists and a significant body of research-based outcome studies suggest that behavioral MFT is quite successful in promoting and maintaining change (30). As in insight-oriented MFT, there are many different approaches to promoting behavioral change in relationships (Table 2–3). Although these different approaches represent major stylistic differences, they nonetheless "hit the ball" in the same way.

Some of the approaches briefly described below are behavioral in that they depend on various aspects of the behavior-exchange model; others are behavioral in that they focus on changing the way people interact; and still others are behavioral in that they provide information about the problem, about various options for solving the problem, or about communication and other skills. All are behavioral approaches, and all depend on the principle that behavior change precedes affective change.

Structural Family Therapy

Salvador Minuchin at the Philadelphia Child Guidance Clinic developed a model of family therapy based on his understanding of the structure of the family (31). This structural approach focuses on both the hierarchy of relationships in the family and the rules of relating that define the boundaries between the subsystems of the family. In structural therapy the recursive nature of the transactions is used to intuit the rules of the system; this information in turn helps clarify the structure of the system.

By attending to the structure of the family and designing interventions to modify the structure, Minuchin and his followers have been able to treat some of the most entrenched, multiproblem families. These families often have little psychological insight and present with some of the most difficult psychosomatic problems, such as anorexia nervosa (32).

TABLE 2–3. **Behavioral marital and family therapy approaches**

Approach	Founder(s)	Intervention focus
Structural	Minuchin	Alteration of the hierarchy, rules, and boundaries in relationships
Strategic	Haley	Interruption of repetitive and maladaptive interactional patterns
Brief	Watzlawick et al. Selvini-Palazzoli	Family strategies for solving problems and communicating
Solution focused	de Shazer	Practical modifications to problem-solving process
Behavioral	Jacobson and Margolin	Behavioral exchange and rational bargains that lead to new social learning
Psychoeducational	Goldstein and Miklowitz	Targeted information

Working from a behavioral standpoint, structural family therapists map the interpersonal dynamics of a family by focusing on the interpersonal transactions that create the psychological boundaries. They are most interested in the boundaries that separate and distinguish the generations, those that separate and distinguish sibling and the individual subsystems, and those that define the alliances and coalitions within the family.

Structural family therapy introduces form and order into some of the most chaotic and difficult relationships, possibly because focusing on the structure of the family prevents family members as well as the therapist from getting lost in the details of the very serious problems of entrenched families. Once form and order are established, a wide range of clinical symptoms may abate; even some biochemical parameters, such as blood sugar in persons with insulin-dependent (brittle) diabetes, can revert toward normal.

Strategic Family Therapy

Working from a systems-based model, Jay Haley (33) and other strategic therapists suggest that understanding, emotions, and transference have no place in relationship therapy. Instead, they propose that it is the repetitive and maladaptive interactional patterns that need to be changed. They pay no particular attention to the cause. Although the therapist must understand these patterns from the perspective of being able to define them, merely understanding the cause of the patterns may be considered worse than "not useful"; it can even be thought of as counterproductive. Strategic therapists will often exclude the family or couple from knowing the details of the perceived patterns or intervention tactics.

Haley and his followers developed a host of ingenious techniques for modifying maladaptive interactional patterns. These strategic interventions, often combined with structural interventions, are particularly useful when families are entrenched in a particular point of view or are negatively disposed toward therapy. A family in a constant state of uproar may, for example, be instructed to continue fighting, but only at prescribed times or on prescribed days. Following this prescription changes nothing yet changes everything, because the very act of deciding when to fight introduces order and forethought to the chaotic picture.

Like the structural therapist, the strategic therapist strives to change only the behavior—confident that affective change, feelings of closeness, and the ability to solve problems will change along the way. Some of Haley's ideas draw on the work of Milton Erickson. Erickson's genius as a therapist lay in his ability to invent interventions that bypassed rather than confronted a person's defenses. Haley and the strategic therapists make good use of the idea of using creative, often paradoxical prescriptions. The Ericksonian therapists, generally considered to be strategic therapists, find ways to deliver these prescriptions to the entire family through the use of metaphor and trance (34).

Brief Family Therapy

Brief family therapy, as it is known, has been a work-in-process since the earliest days of family therapy. Long before it was either fashionable or mandated by health insurance and HMO treatment cost-containing strategies, the brief family therapists at the Mental Research Institute in Palo Alto (also known as the Palo Alto Group) experimented with and refined techniques for completing therapy within 10 sessions. Working from an orthodox systems approach, they attended to the way a family solves its problems rather than to the reasons for the problem or the individual pathology that may be present (35). Their model expands a communications-based approach founded in cybernetics. Practical and solution-oriented, the approach and techniques of the Palo Alto Group's model are a cornerstone of what is now thought of as brief therapy. This model, with its focus on the regulation of family patterns by the family rules, represents one of the purely systems-based approaches.

The Milan school, an outgrowth of the Palo Alto Group's model, presents another example of a pure systems approach. Developed by Selvini-Palazzoli, this approach examines every aspect of the present relationship, focusing on the way each person tries to help the family (36). In this model even the most outrageous behavior can be framed in a positive light by bringing the behavior under the umbrella of helping the family. This approach creates a situation in which it is very difficult for family members to maintain unwanted patterns.

Both the Palo Alto Group and the Milan School approaches also promote the idea of *cotherapy* and the use of therapist teams, with in-room teams and teams behind one-way screens working together. The influence of this group of family therapists can be felt in every MFT setting.

Solution-Focused Therapy

The brief family therapy approach led naturally to the development of solution-focused approaches to family therapy. Again, the format is brief therapy, and the attitude is entirely present-centered. The interventions are typically strategic, and, most important, the philosophy and techniques are usually quite practical. Not surprisingly, solution-focused approaches (37) have found a home in the current managed-care environment.

The solution-focused approaches, like brief therapy approaches, work best in high-functioning families that are relatively flexible, as compared with firmly entrenched ones. They also work best when the family or couple already have some skills to manage their own lives. Both solution-focused and brief therapy may be usefully combined with psychoeducational, behavioral, and other forms of therapy that lead to the acquisition of needed skills.

Behavioral Marital Family Therapy

Within the entire category of behavioral MFT is a specific approach, also called *behavioral marital family therapy,* that uses a behavioral-exchange model, in which is postulated the existence of a storehouse of items each of us wants: love, sex, status, and life support. We trade with each other for these commodities, and the nature of the trade defines the relationship. For most families and couples, the store is relatively closed—that is, all the goodies are in the same location, and each exchange affects other exchanges (38).

Behavior-exchange theory helps us to understand both the properties and the context of interpersonal relationships by placing them into a framework of the rational bargains that partners make. Such an understanding leads directly to a social-learning approach to facilitating improved relations. Behaviorally oriented relationship therapists help families in ways such as identifying antecedent events; structuring agreements; teaching the principles of reinforcement and, in certain circumstances, the use of punishment (aversive conditioning); and anticipating and planning for possible sources of stress in the future. These approaches are particularly useful when school-age children are involved and conduct problems predominate. They are also useful in certain marital situations, such as when there is sexual dysfunction or when marriage enrichment is the primary goal.

Psychoeducational Approaches

One of the most significant recent developments in the field has been recognition of the role of educational approaches in treating and managing serious mental illness and in helping families when a family member has a chronic illness. Although it is common for relationship therapists to incorporate educational components into their approach, the current data suggest definite benefits for many families when a comprehensive educational program is instituted early in the course of treatment.

There are three main psychoeducational approaches: Parent Management Training, Relapse Prevention Training, and Family Group Education. Detailed protocols are available for these approaches for use with parents who have a child with conduct disorder and with families in which a family member has a chronic disability, is hospitalized for schizophrenia, or has a severe substance abuse problem. These protocols have been subjected to rigorous testing and have proven to be quite valuable.

Parent Management Training

Parent Management Training is a form of behavior therapy through which parents of a child with conduct disorder are trained to be therapists for their child; in the process, they develop a new set of parenting skills. Parents learn to recognize and assess problem behaviors and how to apply various social-learning procedures such as positive reinforcements, contingency contracting, aversive conditioning, and other techniques. As part of the process, the teaching methods included are ones the parents will themselves use with the child: modeling, role playing, contracting, feedback, and practice, among others. Parent Management Training has proven valuable in helping families in which a child has either conduct disorder or autism. It has also proven to be of some help for children with attention-deficit/hyperactivity disorder. It has been less effective when the child has an anxiety disorder (39, 40).

Relapse Prevention Training

Based on the recent review by Goldstein and Miklowitz (41), it was concluded that relapse prevention training programs can reduce the relapse rate for patients with psychotic disorders. Although this was a very specific review, it seems likely that the family education protocol approach can be applied to substance abuse and other severe but nonpsychotic disorders. This is particularly relevant when psychosocial stressors are known to play a significant role in the course of the illness.

One set of guidelines for organizing psychoeducational interventions when a family member has a serious mental illness requires that the therapist understand the impact of the disorder on the family and the way the family's response supports the maintenance of the symptom. Some families expect more of the individual than is realistic, whereas others expect too little and therefore hinder progress. Often families also fear change. Fortunately, families can be taught to respond differently.

Goldstein and Miklowitz believe that the following issues are especially critical in formulating a psychotherapeutic program:

- Integration of the psychotic experience
- Acceptance of vulnerability to future episodes
- Acceptance of dependence on psychotropic medications for symptom control
- Anticipation of the stressful life events that act as triggers for recurrence of the disorders
- Ability to distinguish personality traits from symptoms of the disorder

They also concluded that it is important to engage the family of the psychotic patient early in the process in order to educate them about the illness, make specific recommendations for coping, communication, and problem solving, and prepare them for early crisis intervention.

Family Group Education

Family Group Education—which was specifically devised as family-centered interventions for people with chronic disabilities—uses an eight-session, multiple-family discussion group format. In this program, instructional presentations are followed by group discussion. The group-interaction component is developed through use of the instructional material or other disability-related information (42).

■ INTEGRATIVE MODELS

In recent years, several new relationship therapy models have been developed that combine different elements of the various scholastic models into a cohesive unit. There are many different routes to integration (43, 44). One could, for example, combine elements of strategic and structural models, using a theoretical framework for integration. Alternatively, one could combine systems and individual approaches, attending instead to different strategies.

Integrative approaches are particularly common to the treatment of severe mental illness and chronic illness, in which the biologic, the behavioral, and the educational are all programmatically integrated (42). There are several possible advantages to integrating elements of the different approaches; the main advantage is flexibility with respect to both patient needs and therapist comfort. We have already discussed the Bader and Pearson developmental model (18) and Bowen's multigenerational model (21) as examples of integration that combines the individual and the system. We present a third model, Redecision Relationship Therapy, in Chapter 4.

■ REFERENCES

1. Broderick C, Schrader S: The history of professional marriage and family therapy, in Handbook of Family Therapy, Vol II. Edited by Gurman AS, Kniskern DP. New York, Brunner/Mazel, 1991, pp 3–40
2. Wynne LC, Singer MT: Pseudo-mutuality in the family relations of schizophrenics. Arch Gen Psychiatry 9:161–206, 1963
3. Leff JP, Vaughn CE: Expressed Emotion in Families: Its Significance for Mental Illness. New York, Guilford, 1985
4. Hoffman L: Foundations of Family Therapy: A Conceptual Framework for Systems Change. New York, Basic Books, 1981, pp 105–125
5. Reiss D: Varieties of consensual experience. Fam Process 10:1–35, 1971
6. Gilligan C: In a Different Voice. Cambridge, MA, Harvard University Press, 1982
7. Goldner V: Generation and gender: normative and covert hierarchies. Fam Process 27:17–31, 1988
8. Philpot C, Brooks G: Intergender communication and gender-sensitive family therapy, in Integrating Family Therapy: Handbook of Family Psychology and Systems Theory. Edited by Mikesell R, Lusterman D,

McDaniel C. Washington, DC, American Psychological Association, 1995, pp 303–326

9. Walker L: The Battered Woman. New York, Harper & Row, 1985
10. Miller J: Toward a general theory for the behavioral sciences. Am Psychol 10:695–704, 1955
11. Snyder D, Wills R, Grady-Fletcher A: Long-term effectiveness of behavioral versus insight-oriented marital therapy: a 4-year follow-up study. J Consult Clin Psychol 59:138–141, 1991
12. Ackerman NW: Family psychotherapy and psychoanalysis: the implications of difference. Fam Process 1:30–43, 1962
13. Slipp S: Object Relations: A Dynamic Bridge Between Individual and Family Treatment. New York, Jason Aronson, 1984
14. Kadis L, McClendon R: Redecision family therapy: its use with intensive multiple family groups. American Journal of Family Therapy 9:75–83, 1981
15. Paul N, Paul B: A Marital Puzzle: Transgenerational Analysis in Marriage. New York, WW Norton, 1975
16. Stierlin H: Separating Parents and Adolescents: A Perspective on Running Away, Schizophrenia, and Waywardness. New York, Quadrangle/New York Times, 1974
17. Framo J: Family of origin as a therapeutic resource for adults in marital and family therapy: you can and should go home again. Fam Process 15:193–210, 1980
18. Bader E, Pearson P: In Quest of the Mythical Mate. New York, Brunner/Mazel, 1988
19. Scharff D, Scharff JS: Object Relations Family Therapy. New York, Jason Aronson, 1986
20. Givelber F: Object relations and the couple: separation-individuation, intimacy and marriage, in One Couple, Four Realities: Multiple Perspectives on Couples Therapy. Edited by Chasin R, Grunebaum H, Herzig M. New York, Guilford, 1990, pp 171–190
21. Bowen M: Family Therapy in Clinical Practice. New York, Jason Aronson, 1978
22. Friedman D: Bowen theory and therapy, in Handbook of Family Therapy, Vol II. Edited by Gurman AS, Kniskern DP. New York, Brunner/Mazel, 1991, pp 134–170
23. McGoldrick M, Gerson R: Genograms in Family Assessment. New York, WW Norton, 1985

24. Boszormenyi-Nagy I, Spark GM: Invisible Loyalties: Reciprocity in Intergenerational Family Therapy. New York, Harper & Row, 1973

25. Anderson H, Goolishian H: Human systems as linguistic systems: preliminary and evolving ideas about the implications for clinical theory. Fam Process 27:371–393, 1988

26. Hoffman L: Constructing realities: an art of lenses. Fam Process 29:1–12, 1990

27. White M, Epston D: Narrative Means to Therapeutic Ends. New York, WW Norton, 1990

28. Satir V: Conjoint Family Therapy. Palo Alto, CA, Science and Behavior Books, 1964 [3rd Edition, 1983]

29. Napier AY, Whitaker CA: The Family Crucible. New York, Harper & Row, 1978

30. Jacobson N, Addis M: Research on couples and couple therapy: What do we know? Where are we going? Special Section: Couples and couple therapy. J Consult Clin Psychol 61:85–93, 1993

31. Minuchin S, Montalvo B, Guerney B, et al: Families of the Slums: An Exploration of Their Structure and Treatment. New York, Basic Books, 1967

32. Minuchin S, Rosman B, Baker L: Psychosomatic Families: Anorexia Nervosa in Context. Cambridge, Harvard University Press, 1978

33. Haley J: Problem-Solving Therapy: New Strategies for Effective Family Therapy. San Francisco, CA, Jossey-Bass, 1976

34. Lankton S, Lankton C: Tales of Enchantment: Goal-Oriented Metaphors for Adults and Children in Therapy. New York, Brunner/Mazel, 1989

35. Watzlawick P, Weakland JH, Fisch R. Change: Principles of Problem Formation and Problem Resolution. New York, WW Norton, 1974

36. Selvini-Palazzoli M, Boscolo L, Cecchin G, et al: Hypothesizing-circularity-neutrality. Fam Process 19:3–12, 1980

37. de Shazer S: Clues: Investigating Solutions in Brief Therapy. New York, WW Norton, 1988

38. Jacobson N, Margolin G: Marital Therapy: Strategies Based on Social Learning and Behavior Exchange Principles. New York, Brunner/Mazel, 1979

39. Estrada A, Pinsof W: The effectiveness of family therapies for selected behavioral disorders of childhood. Journal of Marital and Family Therapy 21:403–440, 1995

40. Kazdin AE: Treatment of conduct disorder: progress and directions in psychotherapy research. Development and Psychopathology 5:277–310, 1993

41. Goldstein M, Miklowitz D: The effectiveness of psychoeducational family therapy in the treatment of schizophrenic disorders. Journal of Marital and Family Therapy 21:361–376, 1995

42. Gonzalez S, Steinglass P, Reiss D: Putting the illness in its place: discussion groups for families with chronic medical illnesses. Fam Process 28:69–87, 1989

43. Perlmutter R: A Family Approach to Psychiatric Disorders. Washington, DC, American Psychiatric Press, 1996

44. Lebow J: The integrative revolution in couple and family therapy. Fam Process 36:1–18, 1997

PART II

THE PRACTICE OF
RELATIONSHIP THERAPY

3

TEN GUIDELINES AND TECHNIQUES FOR PRACTICE

Relationships are unique—each and every one of them. No single set of skills or any total theory can possibly apply to them all. Nevertheless, a growing body of evidence indicates that a planned approach to treatment is necessary for positive change to occur and is key to a successful outcome.

Current research has outlined two elements that must be present in relationship therapy for positive change to occur in a reasonable period of time and for this change to endure: 1) a definite focus to the therapy and 2) a clear connection between presenting problems and the associated feelings, childhood experiences, and cognitive processing. Neither insight nor expressing feelings is sufficient alone to produce durable change; both are essential.

Many theories and ways of thinking about the dilemma of relationships contribute elements that can guide us in creating therapy regimens that are both efficient and effective. In this chapter we incorporate information from current scholastic theories, strategies, and techniques within a set of 10 general guidelines that help frame the entire field of relationship therapy (Table 3–1). In the next chapter we present, in some detail, our own integrated treatment model, Redecision Relationship Therapy (RRT). It was chosen not only because of its obvious familiarity to us but also because the model has a structure that allows for flexibility in its application and demonstrates ways to combine the different approaches.

To make this truly a *concise* guide to marital and family therapy, we present the 10 guidelines as practical suggestions for working with relationships. In this chapter we cover the nuts and bolts, the "How To Do It," of relationship therapy. We begin by considering the particular therapist's attitude and theoretical orientation and continue through the first to the last contacts with the patient family or couple. These 10 general guidelines apply to relationship therapy regardless of the presenting problem of the couple or family, the personality or theoretical background of the therapist, or the cultural context of the family or couple.

■ GUIDELINE 1: BE SOLIDLY BASED IN THEORY

Throughout this book we have been talking, and will continue to talk, about how relationships can be changed. In a nutshell, we believe that enduring change occurs when the relational difficulties in the present—the observable here and now—are connected to the individuals' beliefs about themselves—the past—and that changes in beliefs about the self are then made relevant to the future—from the present to the past and "back to the future." This process of

---

TABLE 3–1. **Ten guidelines for relationship therapy**

1. Be solidly based in theory.
2. Be committed to a relationship approach.
3. Understand how individuals change.
4. Make contact.
5. Acquire and organize data about the system.
6. Form therapeutic contracts.
7. Make interventions into the system.
8. Acquire and organize data about the individual.
9. Make individual changes.
10. Create new and healthy relationship systems.

changing relationships also requires additional elements; a solid theoretical base, the first guideline, is essential to relationship therapy.

Why is a solid theoretical base important? Like contracts, a solid theoretical base frames the therapy. It both prescribes and proscribes the way we see things, say things, and structure interventions. This consistency of a theoretical base also provides an element of safety for the patient. The choice of a particular relationship theory is not as important to the success of the therapy as is a solid grounding in theory.

Consistency with regard to how the therapist will operate is also important, no matter what his or her theoretical orientation may be. This process begins with

1. Seeing and hearing what's actually occurring in the here and now, in the interactions or process of the family or couple.

The process continues with the therapist

2. Experiencing the impact of what he or she is seeing and hearing;
3. Interpreting the information from a consistent theoretical frame of reference;
4. Defining the new outcomes that need to happen for positive change to occur;
5. Making a plan for achieving the new outcome; and, finally,
6. Executing the plan.

■ GUIDELINE 2: BE COMMITTED TO A RELATIONSHIP APPROACH

The relationship therapist uses systems thinking while including elements of both individual and group dynamics. In this way, he or she looks first at the forest and then at the trees, deciding at any moment in time which perspective will take precedence.

Systems thinking is about changing patterns. Even when the individual (one piece within the pattern) is the focus, the emphasis is on how this individual fits into the whole. Sometimes the family or couple dynamics that are being played out in the office tend to overwhelm the therapist, but, when the therapist is committed to seeing the whole, it becomes possible to fit the individual pieces into the totality of the picture. Systems thinking allows for the shift from thinking about the parts to thinking about the whole. It provides a way to see beyond current events to the forces that have created the problems and also the forces that can shape positive future change for individuals and the family.

The complex concepts relevant to understanding systems can be boiled down to a few basic principles that work equally well in family, couple, and organizational settings (Table 3–2):

1. The problems presented today in the relationship therapist's office are a result of a family's or a couple's solutions of yesterday. Relationship therapists have long known and accepted that the presenting problem is not in fact the problem; instead, it is the way the family has gone about solving the presenting problem and other difficulties that is the real problem. What worked best in adapting to and managing the early childhood environment—what helped us feel safe and the environment seem predictable—are the solutions of yesterday and function as a barrier within the present relationship.

TABLE 3–2. **Guiding principles for systems thinking**

1. Today's relationship problems are the result of yesterday's solutions.
2. "Quick fixes" can make the underlying problem worse.
3. The harder a system is pushed, the harder it resists.
4. Cause and effect may not be closely related in time.
5. A change in any part of the system will create change in other parts.

Source. Adapted from Senge (1).

2. Fixing the symptoms of the problem may bring immediate relief, but the "quick fix" approach enriches the soil for the problem's roots to go deeper and multiply beneath the surface. The ostensible "cure" can quickly become worse than the disease. For example, it is possible to teach a mother and her teenage daughter to negotiate a mutually agreeable curfew that could resolve their current dilemma. Such an approach might, however, make a systemic problem—for example, the father's exclusion—worse.

3. Because of the feedback and balancing properties of systems, the harder a system is pushed, the harder it resists or pushes back. This everyday phenomenon is demonstrated in a typical response to homework given in the therapy setting. In spite of the family's general agreement with the goals of the assignment, and a clear understanding of the specific tasks involved, the family may fail to follow through. Frequently, the family is reluctant because completing the assignment would likely result in a change. The bigger the potential change, the more difficult it will be to complete the assignment.

4. Cause and effect are not necessarily closely related in time. Systems thinking considers what effects a decision will have in the long term as well as what it will bring in the immediate future. Incorporating the capacity for change has the slow, evolving caliber of time-lapse photography rather than the relatively instantaneous quality of taking a snapshot. Systems thinking implicitly carries with it a long-range planning perspective.

5. A change in one part of the system has a wide-ranging impact and will effect changes in all other parts of the system. If an individual family member changes, the complex pattern of interaction will necessarily change in some way.

In addition to using systems thinking, the relationship therapist is committed to creating a safe, involved, interactive, and even fun environment that fosters participation. Moving a family or couple into participation is essential because without participation there is no relationship therapy. Creating participation means supporting the accountability and dignity of every person in the family regardless of age, sex, or role. It also means encouraging learning and sharing so that all those involved in the therapy will express what they know, what they feel, and who they are.

A safe environment occurs when there is a contract that explicitly establishes the meaning of safety in therapy. Sometimes there must even be rules to protect against negative consequences to family members because of what they have brought up within a therapy session. For instance, it is not unusual for siblings to "get" each other later because they "were told on"; for partners to use therapy material against each other when in the midst of battle; or for parents to be punitive with their children for revealing family secrets. Any violation of safety becomes the first order of business at the next therapy session. Again, without safety, relationship therapy simply cannot work.

The relationship therapist needs to be an exceptionally good listener, making it as easy as possible for a family's patterns as well as the individuals in the family to reveal themselves. The listening component of relationship therapy is slightly different from that of individual therapy. In relationship therapy what is *seen* is usually more important than what is *heard*—especially when they don't match. Listening with the "third ear" is a focused form of attention to listen for "what happens first, and what happens next, and then what leads to the next interaction." It is also hearing what wasn't said and is missing, as well as what was said, to whom, and in what tone of voice. Seeing with the "third eye" is noticing the nonverbal responses of each family or couple member. Noting when Johnny is in the corner with the toys is a way of making contact with him. Relationship therapists know that listening to Johnny or Suzie sometimes means that they get on the floor with the ball or crayons. It also means commenting on Suzie's pink plastic purse with the orange flowers and green zipper or Johnny's lost tooth.

Very crucially, the relationship therapist emphasizes the strengths and resources of the relationship and the individuals. Keeping a positive focus encourages participation. It allows individuals to reveal themselves, even though this is a most difficult thing in the relationship and in the context of relationship therapy. It supports relationship loyalty and thereby facilitates problem solving and behavioral change. When a positive focus is maintained, family and couple teams are motivated to learn and change together, instead of blaming, dividing, and undermining.

Furthermore, the relationship therapist is ready and available to see himself or herself as resourceful and integral, but as a facilitator rather than a central figure in the process that enables families and couples to change. The relationship therapist's job involves assisting people not only with taking responsibility for their own change but also with understanding, helping, and crediting others within the relationship system. Mending the relationship is what is important, not the therapist's role in that process.

Finally, relationship therapy is an ever-active therapy. Inactivity is like treading water during sessions and usually magnifies relationship problems. This can quickly lead to discouragement with the therapy process.

■ GUIDELINE 3: UNDERSTAND HOW INDIVIDUALS CHANGE

A therapist, of course, ideally brings to every treatment situation considerable knowledge derived from years of training, experience, and deep thinking about the phenomenon of personal transformation. One of the most crucial aspects of practice-oriented wisdom is an understanding of and appreciation for the process of positive change that must take place if therapy is going to be successful.

The caricature of the woman dragging her resisting husband into the therapist's office points to a problem frequently underlying relationship therapy. More often than not, only one member of the relationship system is ready and willing to make whatever changes may be necessary. The other partner in a couple or other family members who are not ready to make the changes that need to be made to resolve a specific problem may, in fact, strongly resist making them. But it is also quite true that often the caricatured woman doing the dragging is ready only to the extent that she wants the relationship therapist to "fix" the reluctant partner, since she assumes that he alone has created the problem. Be that as it may, when the relationship is the problem, the difference in readiness between the partners or other family members is an important issue and often makes the presenting problem seem insurmountable, and this further heightens the distress.

Helping couples and families change might be likened to aiding them first to consider the relationship as a team and then to improve their team performance. To do this well, a therapist must be acquainted with the process of individual change and, beyond that, understand the impact of individual change on the "team" of the family or couple.

When the therapist labels the person who is not ready for relationship therapy as being "resistant," when family members complain of his or her lack of motivation, or when peer counselors or other mental health professionals talk in terms of the person's being "in denial," the reluctant position often becomes hardened.

Over the past several years researchers have investigated the phenomenon of *readiness for change* (2). Examining change across many different health-related behaviors, they have developed a model for evaluating an individual's readiness for change. A patient is asked to list the possible benefits of therapy as well as the negative aspects, and the ratio of pros to cons (or cons to pros) then provides a simple measure of progress. In the earliest stage of the change process, when the patient is unlikely even to be aware of the basic problem, the cons may outweigh the pros. But as the patient moves through the stages, this ratio reverses until the pros significantly outweigh the cons.

Business leaders have also looked at the principles for "taking charge of change" (3). The results of these investigations suggest that readiness for change is one of the most important determinants of outcome in the change process. Recognition of this is especially relevant for therapy, since 40% of the potential patients—family members who are "dragged" into therapy—are not even sure a problem exists; these are the couples or families with the highest dropout rates.

Whatever explanation or theory may be used to explain the process of change itself, it is clear that patients must first arrive at an understanding of the need for change, as well as develop the desire to change, before they can accomplish their goals. Often, as mentioned, one or more members of the family or couple reluctantly enter the relationship therapy process and are not even able to recognize and acknowledge the existence of any serious problem. Other family members, on the other hand, may be totally unwilling or else discouraged when confronted by the prospect of either participating in the change process, changing something in themselves, or having the relationship somehow altered when their partner or another family member changes. In couple therapy, for instance, it is common for Partner A to say, "He drinks too much," and then for Partner B to respond, "I don't know what he/she is talking about." In families, siblings often don't know what the problem is with Bobby; and, more important, they don't want to know, if it means being dragged into treatment.

A view of the change process is summarized in Table 3–3. By knowing this process, a therapist can see what people need to have before they are able to make changes in the way they interact.

TABLE 3–3. **The change process: what people need**

An awareness and understanding of the need for change
An interest in change, and the desire to effect change
The skills for changing
A plan for changing
Support during the change process
Positive reinforcement for change

Prochaska describes a form of stage-specific therapy and measures success in terms of movement through the stages rather than outcome (2). People must move through each of the stages to reach their goal. Additionally, it is often necessary to recycle through the early stages of the process before gaining the momentum to complete the essential change. The stages of change described by Prochaska are summarized in Table 3–4 and are outlined more specifically below.

In the beginning stage of the change process, *precontemplation,* the goal is to help each person develop an awareness and understanding of the problem. Each family or couple member needs to take partial ownership of the problem through understanding that when anyone in a relationship has a problem, everyone has a problem. The problems of others inevitably impact each person in the family, often not in ways that are apparent until treatment is successfully launched.

Next, in the *contemplation* stage, it is necessary to stimulate interest and desire to participate in the change process. The overall goal is to help individuals recognize that change is needed, and will happen, if relationships are to improve rather than deteriorate further. Thus, it is essential for the therapist to educate patients not just about the problem itself but also about what will be different after the problem is resolved. Many people are frightened about the unknown—about how things will be different when change occurs.

TABLE 3–4.　**Stages of change**

Precontemplation

Contemplation

Preparation

Action

Maintenance

Termination

Source.　Adapted from Prochaska and DiClemente (2).

For instance, one partner in a couple is frequently concerned that the other person will no longer love him/her if either or both of them somehow change.

As people in this stage weigh the pros and cons of change, they need support, gentle nudging, information, and alternative ways to look at things. It is important to define both the problem and the anticipated results so that people become convinced that the negative aspects of the problem to be solved far outweigh their concerns about changing. To make therapy work, they need to make a firm decision to take action on solving the problem.

In the next stage, the *preparation* stage, patients further develop an understanding of the basic problem. Concurrently, the therapist prepares for the therapeutic work to be done by determining whether the persons involved have the minimal capabilities to make the necessary changes. People may not currently have the skills needed to stop smoking, lose weight, be better parents, or allow for more intimacy; but they must have the ability to learn.

During the preparation stage, the therapist determines the trouble spots and develops understanding about what needs to be done to get through them. He or she defines what efforts will be required for the journey and has a plan to manage the difficult points. Good assessment skills are needed to make this appraisal. Having a solid theoretical model of change is also basic.

Working together, the therapist and family members next create a plan of action and set up one or several explicit goals. Without a plan for converting understanding and good intentions into action, people will be unable to learn the skills needed to make the changes. In some therapy models (such as RRT), this preparation stage ends with the *contract,* the mutual agreement between patient and therapist that frames the work to be done in the action stage.

The next stage of the change process is the *action* stage. Individuals in action are looking for what is needed to help them view themselves and others differently. They are ready to experience the pain and joy of changing and have committed both the time and the energy that is needed to feel, think, and behave differently with themselves and with others. Action involves the overt modification of internal and external environments. Taking action is the working stage of the therapy process and requires the courage and support of system members.

Finally, in the *maintenance,* or reinforcement, stage, individual and systemic changes must be strengthened through reinforcement in order to prevent relapse and consolidate gains. In this stage, new learning is practiced and reinforced through positive feedback. Families and couples often need help learning how to stroke—express recognition for—and support one another. They also need to learn how to keep their relationships healthy and functioning and to develop the family and individual resilience necessary to successfully live in today's world.

Termination is the last stage of the therapeutic change process. At this stage new individual behaviors and new system patterns are integrated into the relationships and the therapeutic contacts are completed.

Assessing the readiness for therapy is a valuable adjunct to the therapist's armamentarium. It provides a way to understand what is commonly thought of as resistance without blaming the patient. In this framework, each person's needs can be understood and met without one person feeling coerced or colluded against. Research on the change process also reminds us that change takes time and hard work—something we may tend to forget.

■ GUIDELINE 4: MAKE CONTACT

There is a distinction between making the initial contact with the patient family in a telephone or face-to-face conversation and making contact in the therapeutic sense. Here we address contact in both senses.

The Initial Contact

We begin with the initial contact about the patient family. The first inquiry regarding the probable need for relationship therapy is made to a therapist either by an outside referral source or by an individual member of the family. When someone other than a prospective patient, such as a school counselor or a probation officer, calls the therapist, the therapist asks for a general, professionally objective description of the problem and then waits for a family member to initiate direct contact.

In the initial phone contact with a family member, the relationship therapist gathers some basic information:

- A general description of the problem to be addressed in therapy
- The reason(s) that the family or couple has decided to look at this problem now
- Who is directly involved in the problem
- Who is impacted by the problem (this information may not always correlate with who is living at home)

It is also necessary to discuss the business of therapy itself, such as fees, insurance, and scheduling restrictions. After this information is mutually agreed on, the initial interview time is scheduled.

The therapist and the family mutually decide who will attend the first session. This is an extremely important, and in some cases a very difficult, determination. In general, the therapist begins with the proposal that everyone living at home will come in for the initial session, but he or she is ready to modify this position according to the circumstances, remembering that all families and couples are unique. Many parents, for instance, are reluctant to bring in their kids until they have checked out the therapist, to make sure things will be safe. On the other hand, some parents are willing to bring in only the "problem kid" and attempt to shield other family members, including spouses. When the presenting problem relates to an adolescent, it is sometimes important to see the adolescent alone initially so that the therapist is less likely to be perceived as a parent's ally.

Of course, with every situation imaginable occurring in systems or relationship therapy, there are always other ways to look at things. The therapist must be ever alert to any reluctance on a family's or couple's part, so that he or she can respond flexibly to setting up the initial session. Even more than with individual therapy, it is important to meet relationships on their terms, particularly at the start.

The Therapeutic Contact

The initial patient contact generates first impressions and allows the therapist to formulate tentative hypotheses. *Therapeutic* contact is very different. The first session of relationship therapy is often thought of as one of contact, contact, and more contact. As has been aptly said, "Contact is the lifeblood for growth, the means for changing oneself and one's experience of the world. . . . Through contact . . . one does not have to try to change; change simply occurs" (4, p. 101).

For relationship therapy to progress productively, each and every family member needs to be regarded as important, and helped to feel important, within the family system. Five-year-old Sarah; 14-year-old James; Dr. Boris and his wife Flora, 45 and 46 years old, respectively—all are equal in the eyes of the relationship therapist. When this principle is operating during the initial contact, the therapy has begun successfully.

It is hard to say enough about the importance of contact to the process of therapy, regardless of the theoretical orientation. Minuchin, for example, made contact one of the cornerstones of structural therapy, calling it "joining" (5). Watching video clips of the master therapists at work confirms the idea that, whether or not they explicitly say so, part of their gift is their ability to make contact. Contact is very important in other regards as well. Couples often come into therapy complaining about the lack of contact—either explicitly when they talk about avoidance behavior or implicitly when they despair of not being heard or not being understood. Similarly, parents and children complain about not being heard and not being understood.

As part of successful therapy, people learn how to make satisfying contact with each other. They learn to recognize and value each other's uniqueness as individuals and to recognize and value the differences between people. This is the essence of contact. The relationship therapist who is successful—in acknowledging the uniqueness of the participants in therapy, in confronting the frequent attempts patients make to blur the distinctions between themselves and family members, and in valuing each person for who they are—is both making contact and teaching the process of making contact.

During the first visit the relationship therapist is already acquiring systemic data and beginning to make some sense of what is happening. Regardless of the methods one uses as assessment techniques, it is important in the first session to find out what happens in the system when things go well—and what happens when things go poorly.

Four practical suggestions for conducting each session of relationship psychotherapy are listed in Table 3–5.

■ GUIDELINE 5: ACQUIRE AND ORGANIZE SYSTEMS DATA

The most important distinguishing factor of relationship therapy has been the shift in the focus of the dialogue about any particular presenting problem from the content—that is, what patients are

---

TABLE 3–5. **Practical suggestions for conducting each session of relationship therapy**

Help each individual stay actively involved in the therapeutic process.

Utilize each individual's strengths.

Make each session self-contained, so that people go away each time having become aware of something about themselves and their relationship.

Keep a constant bridge to everyday living and interaction.

---

telling us—to the interactional process within the family or couple. To understand this paradigm shift, think of the difference between individual diagnosis and systems or relational diagnosis. When an individual diagnosis is made, at least two distinct things are said: 1) there is something amiss within the patient, and 2) correcting what is amiss will end the complaint or symptom. When a systems or relational diagnosis is made, however, two very different things are said: 1) there is something amiss within the pattern of relationships, and 2) when the relationship patterns are changed, the individuals will have the opportunity to heal themselves.

Marital and family therapy is best thought of as a staged process that begins with acquiring the necessary information to make the relational or systems diagnosis. A variety of assessment techniques and tools are available for use in arriving at an understanding of the family system, regardless of one's theoretical orientation.

If the theory about how people change depends on changing the structural dimensions of the family system, the therapist will prefer to use assessment techniques that clarify the existing structure, and then techniques to change that structure for the needed improvement. But if the theory primarily focuses on the way the family solves problems, the therapist must be able both to assess and to intervene in the system as it is reflected along the problem-solution dimension.

As the different theories of family and couple therapy were developed (see Chapter 2), so were groups of parallel techniques based on these theories. In subsequent years, assessment and intervention techniques were tested and then modified. Today, the techniques that were developed in one model are now applied in many, if not all, models of relationship therapy. Because both therapists and families are so variable, the wide availability of different techniques has proven useful. Each therapist has his or her own list of preferred assessment and intervention techniques; families, too, seem more comfortable with different styles of treatment. At the same time, it is important to recognize that in the hands of a creative therapist, a technique primarily used for assessing the nature of the relationship can also become a powerful intervention tool.

Assessment techniques can be classified according to either therapist involvement or approach. When classified according to therapist involvement, assessment techniques form a continuum. At one end are techniques involving complete disengagement, as in the case of the psychologist administering paper-and-pencil tests. In the middle are techniques in which the therapist tries to maintain some degree of neutrality, as when the therapist merely observes the interaction being played out in front of him or her or uses circular questioning for eliciting information about the nature of intrafamilial relationships. At the other end of the continuum are techniques in which the therapist actively choreographs the inter-actions, as when the therapist uses role-playing and coaching techniques common to several schools of family therapy. These techniques will be discussed in more detail later in this chapter in the discussion of Guideline 7.

Assessment techniques can also be classified according to the way the therapist approaches the couple or family. Therapists can be direct or indirect in their approach. Contingent reinforcement techniques tend to be direct, although not necessarily so. Strategic techniques are almost never direct, and many schools of therapy tend to use the paradoxical. Again, flexibility is the key. Therapists themselves are usually more comfortable using one approach or another, depending on both what is familiar and what "works" well for them. Also, different families respond to different approaches, and some problems respond better to one approach than to another.

The choice of assessment and possible intervention techniques, as is evident in the above presentation, is complicated, because no single technique for evaluating the family system stands out as a guaranteed winner. No single strategy has proven uniquely help-ful in conducting systemic assessment. Yet each one can provide useful information.

How one decides which assessment approach to use, and when, is of course part of the art, rather than the science, of relationship therapy. In fact, growing evidence from family therapy outcome studies sug-gests that use of a manual-based approach is a better predictor of a positive outcome than is any other framework (6). If that is true, it stands to reason that developing and following a plan that includes guidelines for which technique to use and when to use it is more likely to result in a positive outcome than is an intuitive, hit-or-miss method.

In summary, acquiring the necessary systems data is an exciting and sometimes monumental task. Typically, a relational diagnosis that does not imply pathology is made as a shorthand description of the interactional patterns. Relational diagnoses can be made either from direct observations of the ongoing process between family members or from inferences about the interactional process developed from collateral data, such as family life cycles, the family genogram, and other indirect reports, to be discussed later in this chapter.

In the concluding part of our discussion of Guideline 5, we take a more extensive look at assessment technologies. We propose two overall categories—direct-observation approaches and self-report approaches—that are defined by the way data are derived (Table 3–6). In direct-observation approaches the therapist observes the system and records data; in self-report approaches the therapist uses self-report forms to obtain data. Of course, approaches from each category are frequently used in combination depending on the goals of the therapeutic design.

TABLE 3–6. **Approaches to relational assessment**

Direct-observation approaches
   Global Assessment of Relational Functioning Scale
   Structured tasks
   Timberlawn model
   Gottman model
   Video and reflecting teams
Self-report approaches
   Family Environment Scale
   Family Adaptation and Cohesion Evaluation Scale
   McMaster's Family Assessment Device

Direct-Observation Approaches

In the direct-observation approaches the therapist creates an observing environment in the office and gathers the necessary information from what is actually seen, heard, and experienced at the moment. The guiding principle behind this idea is that each couple or family will generally reproduce their basic relational patterns as long as it is safe to do so. In family therapy this means that the props to assist accurate direct observation must be available. Materials such as developmentally appropriate toys, paper, and crayons, along with interactional games, are frequently used. (RRT, which is discussed in detail in Chapter 4, primarily uses direct observation as the way to gather data.)

In the clinical setting the direct observer is most often the therapist—a situation with special characteristics to be considered. The observer's mind-set, theoretical orientation, and personal experiences inevitably modify what is seen and how perceptions are processed. A more subtle but equally important factor in observing families comes from the world of theoretical physics. It is well established that what is observed is altered simply by the process of being observed. Therefore, the presence of a third party such as a therapist alters the interactions, and this phenomenon is distinct from the phenomenon of observer bias.

With these caveats in mind, it becomes extremely important to have clear observing criteria. When the rating criteria are well defined and the protocol is firmly established, inter-rater reliability should be sufficiently high enough to ensure the validity and reproducibility of the observations.

We now briefly present some of the more salient direct-observation techniques that are used in assessment.

Global Assessment of Relational Functioning Scale

Recently, the Committee on the Family of the Group for the Advancement of Psychiatry addressed the issue of relational diagnosis and introduced the Global Assessment of Relational Functioning

(GARF) Scale (7, 8) (Table 3–7). This scale assesses three dimensions of family functioning: *joint problem solving,* which focuses on various skills; *organization,* which focuses on role differentiation and maintenance; and *emotional climate.* Although the GARF Scale is relatively new, some early research work suggests that it meets the criteria for validity as an instrument. Since it follows the designs of Axis V of the DSM-IV, the GARF Scale may ultimately prove to be valuable as an overall measure of the health of any relationship under scrutiny.

The GARF Scale is a good example of a direct-observation, systems-oriented assessment instrument. However, the GARF Scale, unlike the Timberlawn Model and the Family Adaptation and Cohesion Evaluation Scale–II (see below), is limited in that although it describes the relationship, it does not inform relationship therapists about how or where to intervene.

Structured Tasks

When families come into the office, they are naturally inclined to focus all their attention on the therapist. They begin by talking directly to him or her, saying things, or else not saying things, supposedly for the therapist's benefit. The therapist's first obligation, therefore, is getting the family to be interactional in the office. This is often accomplished by providing a structured task for the family to do together. The therapist then has the opportunity to sit back and observe, thereby possibly getting a completely different viewpoint of the relationship system than would have been possible had he or she merely listened to what was being said.

Techniques that structure the activity of the family are a standard part of many family and couple therapist's repertoire. These structured activities, used with all ages, range from the simple instructions, such as "Talk with each other for the next few minutes about what the problem is, and I will sit back and listen," to the more elaborate "Here is a large sheet of news print and some crayons. Draw a picture of your family." Games, hand puppets, video

TABLE 3–7. Global Assessment of Relational Functioning (GARF)

Overall	Description of relational unit	Problem solving	Organization	Emotional climate
81–100	Functioning satisfactorily	Agreed on routines	Role agreed on	Open with feelings
61–80	Difficulties not always resolved	Pain and conflict that are not disruptive of routines	Decision making not always competent	Warmth and caring; some emotional blocking
41–60	Occasionally satisfying but dysfunctional	Frequent unresolved conflicts that are sometimes disruptive	Decision making intermittently effective	Emotions interfering with functioning
21–40	Obviously dysfunctional	Routines not meeting needs of members	Decision making ineffective	Frequent distancing and hostility; little enjoyment
1–20	Too dysfunctional for contact and attachment	Routines negligible	Boundaries unrecognizable	Despair and cynicism pervasive

Note. A code of 0 indicates inadequate information.
Source. Adapted with permission from DSM-IV (7).

games, and toys that can be used in a variety of ways (e.g., blocks) are all examples of tools used when creating structured activities. The observations made in the course of the family's participation in playing or working with these tools contribute considerably to the overall assessment of the relationship patterns in the family.

Timberlawn Model

Lewis and Beavers and their colleagues at the Timberlawn Foundation in Dallas, Texas, were among the first researchers to take interest in assessing the psychological health of families (9). They studied families from the perspective of success in coping with the stresses of modern-day life. Families were given standardized tasks that are only slightly different from those previously mentioned in that the families were all asked to "talk together for 10 minutes and plan a family outing," and then they were observed. As the families engaged in the specifically assigned task, individual behaviors and the patterns of interaction were detected. A rating scale was then developed to reliably evaluate power, structure, autonomy, affect, perception of reality, and efficiency in completing tasks among the individuals within the system as well as in the family as a unit. Based on the outcome of these studies, a range of family functioning, from optimal to severely dysfunctional, was described.

Gottman Model

Gottman took a different tack (10). He brought couples into the psychophysiology laboratory, and in a semistructured situation, while they were attached to various psychophysiologic recording devices, he presented them with a task similar to the one described for the Timberlawn group. Both verbal and nonverbal communication sequences were evaluated with standardized rating scales. At the same time, heart rate, blood pressure, facial expressions, and electrogalvanic skin resistance were recorded.

Unlike other assessment approaches, this complete psychophysiologic procedure is not readily accessible in the therapy setting. The rating scales and the conclusions are, however, available and very relevant. For instance, four factors—criticism, contempt, defensiveness, and what was called "stonewalling"—reliably predict which marriages are doomed to fail in the following few years (11).

Video and Reflecting Teams

Several schools of therapy rely on a semistructured interview situation in which there is a formal methodology for observing the family and drawing inferences about the system. Often these structures are also an integral part of the intervention strategy rather than solely a means of gathering data. The use of audio/video feedback related to some structured activity and the introduction of a reflecting team are examples of techniques that are used simultaneously to gather data, encourage family interaction, and intervene in the marital or family system.

Video. Structured activities are conducted under the eye of the video camera, and the resulting videotape is then used by the therapist to review his or her in-room observations and fine-tune the initial hypothesis. Alternatively, the video is used as part of the intervention strategy: the family is given the assignment to view the videotape at home and talk about it in various prescribed formats. How couples and families do or do not complete the assignment, as well as how they integrate the observations, becomes part of the intervention and also feeds back to the next step in therapy.

Immediate review of videotape segments can be turned into a powerful intervention, especially for couples. The couple is asked to act as therapists to the couple on the videotape and to make observations of what they see as the problem and recommendations for resolution of that problem. This intervention, which is an elaboration of the simple feedback technique, allows the couple to get some distance from the emotional struggle and engage their observing egos in problem solving.

Although use of the video camera and videotapes may be extremely valuable, this intervention is not utilized as frequently as it could be because it requires the therapist to also manage the technology during the interview—a significant feat for some therapists.

Reflecting teams. Use of the reflecting team is another variation on the theme of structuring a family interaction, observing the interaction, and then discussing the observations with the family (12). In this approach the family is interviewed by one or two therapists in the room while a "team" (it may only be one person) watches and listens behind the one-way mirror. At some point during the interview (it may occur more than once), the reflecting team comes into the therapy room to report their observations and perhaps to state their hypotheses. This feedback serves as the basis for subsequent discussion.

The reflecting team has been incorporated into several different therapy approaches. Each of these applications has made an important contribution to clinicians' understanding of how to use the team and make sense of the observations.

This form of feedback can have a significant impact on the family. Two experts are better than one, and three or four experts, some of whom are independent observers, are much better than one or two in-room therapists. But there are some potential drawbacks. Families can feel overwhelmed by input from so many therapists. The team can get on the wrong track as well as on the right track. And people in therapy can be easily hurt. Therefore, this technique requires great care.

Self-Report Approaches

Self-administered questionnaires are an important part of most family research protocols. In the clinical setting they are used mainly in the early phase of therapy, when the therapist wants to generate one or more hypotheses about the relationship patterns within the family. Each family member is asked to complete the form in private and return it at the next session. In addition to providing basic information about how individual family members view themselves and their families, self-report questionnaires tend to start family members thinking about themselves and their family in a different way. More often than not, the questions asked on the form have been on people's minds in other ways but have not been verbalized until now. Thus, the task of answering the questionnaire is an intervention in itself and may promote awareness or even change the pattern of interaction. When combined with skillfully implemented feedback of the results, the entire test-taking/feedback experience can be an important event in the course of therapy for the family.

The self-report paper-and-pencil questionnaires are often administered by an assistant to the therapist. In this way, the therapist can remain neutral. When a therapist chooses to administer the test, some neutrality is lost, and this becomes another factor in the therapy setting. The patient's reaction must then be taken into account as part of the evaluation. Some families will work hard to please the therapist, whereas others will begin treating the therapist as an alien force.

The three most frequently used self-report questionnaires are the Family Environment Scale, Family Adaptation and Cohesion Evaluation Scale, and McMaster's Family Assessment Device (and its successors).

Family Environment Scale

The Family Environment Scale (FES) (13) is an empirically derived scale that measures several dimensions of family functioning, with cohesiveness and expressivity being the two most important ones. This scale has proven very useful in screening families in large-scale studies, particularly families in which alcohol plays an important role.

Family Adaptation and Cohesion Evaluation Scale

The Family Adaptation and Cohesion Evaluation Scale (FACES II) (14), like the FES, is an empirically derived scale that addresses and attempts to measure family cohesion. FACES II, however, measures an additional item, *adaptability,* now referred to as *flexibility.* Work with FACES and its more recent elaborations has led to the development of the Circumplex Model that places families within a 16-quadrant grid reflecting these two major systems dimensions, ranging from the chaotically enmeshed to the rigidly disengaged.

McMaster's Family Assessment Device

The Family Assessment Device (FAD), derived from the McMaster's Scale, or the McMaster's Model of Family Function (15), focuses on different aspects of the family's ability to solve problems. Recently, Miller (16) simplified this scale, producing an elegant Likert-type scale with clearly defined anchor points that results in a global rating. This modification of the FAD evaluates problem solving, effectiveness of communication, ability of the family to assign and complete tasks (called "roles" here), behavior control, and a measure, best described as empathy, that includes affective responsiveness and affective involvement.

■ GUIDELINE 6: FORM THERAPEUTIC CONTRACTS

The key to relationship therapy is the *therapeutic contract*: the explicit agreement between the therapist and the individuals who make up the couple or family unit. Contracts center therapy and remind each person of their obligations and objectives. They bring two disparate units, the relationship and the professional, together under the same umbrella and provide them with a common purpose. At the same time, they focus energy, attention, and problem-solving abilities. A clear contract shifts the couple or family into the problem-solving mode. It outlines and supports their strengths, tests their abilities to find solutions, and teaches them how to do it (17).

A contract establishes a boundary that defines the working environment, lays out the work to be done, sets limits on expectations, and both prescribes and proscribes behaviors. With a contract as a point of reference, distractions or interpersonal maneuvering become obvious and then can be explored or handled therapeutically.

Despite their importance, contracts have received little direct attention in the literature. Behavior therapists are most explicit in the way they use contracts. They focus on specific behaviors that the family wants to change and offer specific strategies aimed at changing those behaviors. Structural therapists make an important conceptual leap. They relate dysfunctional behavior to the structure of the family and formulate contracts aimed toward changing the family structure as a way of relieving the symptoms or eliminating the unwanted behaviors. In a similar vein, strategic therapists attempt to integrate the family's view of the problem with their own (the professional's) view of the family's problem-solving strategies. The purpose is to alleviate the symptoms through devising a contract and a strategy for changing the way the family solves the problem.

Another approach (and the one closest to the RRT strategy detailed in the next chapter) is the multilevel contract seen in the work of the Milan school (18). In this approach the family at some point is given a statement that explains the symptom in a way the family can understand, phrases it in positive terms, and addresses each person's view of the family and the problem. Furthermore, this statement, or formulation, brings each person's individual struggle into the context of helping the family.

The goal of the contract-formation process is to arrive at a mutually agreed-on objective that is clearly stated and supported with high motivation for achievement. (Remember that kids eat what they cook, and people support what they create!)

A relationship contract—verbal and/or written—is a blueprint for therapy that is mutually constructed by therapist and patient(s) and includes the six elements outlined in Table 3–8.

The most important task in contract formation is linking up the different levels of the system and getting everyone to work simultaneously toward a common goal or shared vision. To accomplish this task, the therapist must honor individuality, take skeptics seriously and hear their reasons why things won't work (they may be right), and have tactical positive plans for each person in support of the overall relationship plan.

Contracts are the key to successful therapy, and the contracting process as a whole is a major intervention into the relationship system. Within the contracting process, intervention techniques such as reframing and positive connotation are used frequently. These will be discussed more fully in the following section.

■ GUIDELINE 7: MAKE INTERVENTIONS INTO THE SYSTEM

One of the things that makes relationship therapy so challenging, and also fascinating, is the infinite number of ways to intervene in the relationship system. The intervention style and techniques used by relationship therapists are generally dictated by several factors: the presenting problem, the system assessment data, the nature of the therapeutic contract, and, inevitably, the therapist's style and orientation.

TABLE 3–8. **Elements of a relationship contract**

A common understanding of the major complaint

A positive framework stated in ways that each person, regardless of age, can understand

An orientation to the future

A systemic appreciation of the relationship

A way of integrating each family member's unique history and world view

A plan for implementation that can be achieved at the lowest possible self-esteem cost to all involved

---

The clue to choosing an intervention mode is first to try whatever matches the view and theory of the system and then simply to make the intervention in a caring way. As long as the relationship therapist is equally prepared to have his or her original hypothesis proven either right or wrong, the intervention will reveal important systemic information. As much information can be learned from the results of an unsuccessful intervention as from those of a successful one.

In this section we briefly review some of the more standard and popularized intervention techniques. They are set down here only as examples and ideas and not necessarily as models to adopt. Most important, remember that there are innumerable options for intervention and that creativity is the best partner in relationship therapy. Also, as mentioned earlier, each of the assessment approaches, in effect, acts as an intervention strategy. This is because any entry into the system can create change, and any change impacts not one but all parts of the system. It is possible to liken family systems to mobiles; when you move one part, all other parts move accordingly.

We have roughly classified the strategies for intervening in the system into direct and indirect approaches to working with relationship systems. There is some current debate about the value of direct as compared with indirect interventions. If a mother and child are fighting, teaching the mother better approaches to limit setting—a direct intervention—may be useful. This type of intervention addresses the symptom directly, leading to what is called *first-order change.* However, as mentioned previously, systems therapists believe that *second-order change,* a change in the system itself and its rules, is more enduring. In the above example, this might mean stopping the father from interfering in the mother-child relationship, regardless of the context. The goal of most intervention strategies is to interrupt patterns that are nonproductive. This creates opportunities for individuals to distance themselves from their knee-jerk here-and-now reactions and to develop more flexible responses to problem solving. Some of the most important approaches to systems intervention are outlined in Table 3–9.

Direct-Intervention Approaches

Direct interventions are based on assessment information indicating that the relationship system and its individual participants will respond to or comply with direct suggestions, and even instructions, about how to change and reach the defined goals in the most efficient and effective way. Direct interventions assume the cooperation of the family members and rely on their cooperation in order to be effective. Taking advantage of readiness for change, direct interventions derive their power in a cumulative manner, beginning with small steps that combine to lead to overall change.

Communication Techniques

We begin looking at direct-intervention strategies by discussing the communication techniques of active listening and the use of "I" messages. Both of these strategies have become part of our culture. Children are taught them in school, and almost every employee training program teaches interpersonal skills by incorporating

---

TABLE 3–9. **Approaches to systems intervention**

Direct-intervention approaches
  Communication techniques
  Genograms
  Circular questioning
  Role playing and family sculpting
  Environmental interventions
  Homework
Indirect-intervention approaches
  Paradox
  Common understanding techniques
    Reframing
    Positive connotation
    Metaphor and storytelling

---

these two communication techniques. Practice in "I" messages and "active listening" is at the core of most personal-growth experiences, including parent training, marriage enrichment, and a multiplicity of family-oriented programs. Articles explaining these techniques have also appeared in numerous popular magazines and self-help books. Still, despite their widespread popularization, active listening and "I" message communication techniques remain valuable adjuncts in relationship therapy.

Active listening is used to promote structured interaction with a couple or family or to diffuse intense involvement through introduction of a structured paradigm of responses. An example of a therapist's questions for an active-listening structured interaction follows. The example is presented in a generalized format to make the point that this technique is easily applied to many situations.

> "What did you hear him say?"
> "Did she hear you correctly? Is that what you said?"
> "No? Then please say it again."
> "Now what did you hear him say?"
> "Did she get it right?"
> "Okay. Having heard it correctly, what do you think he meant?"
> "Given your interpretation, what do you think and how do you feel?"
> "When you feel _____, how do you behave?"
> "Now, turn and respond directly to _____."

Then the sequence turns to the next person. This technique can be used to teach communication skills, develop understanding, or defuse volatile situations and advance to a problem-solving mode.

"I" messages are a short version of the active-listening technique. They require that each person take responsibility for his or her own actions, feelings, and behavior. The use of "I" messages helps participants to develop an increasing ability to listen, hear,

and then respond to others. They define person-to-person boundaries and support self-development. "I" messages are easily utilized and readily accepted, regardless of the dimensions of the relationship problem.

Furthermore, "I"-message techniques are essential to the evolution of differentiation in the enmeshed couple or family—the couple or family in which individual distinctions are blurred. They promote self-reflecting and the identification of one's own thoughts, feelings, values, needs, and desires, as well as increase awareness of the other family members as separate and distinct individuals.

Genograms

The second most frequently used intervention technique, after the communication techniques described above, is probably the *genogram.* The rationale for the genogram derives from Murray Bowen's belief that an individual's difficulty in managing current relationships results from an incomplete differentiation from the family of origin and that the process of differentiation can be completed by understanding the family of origin in an emotional as well as an intellectual sense.

The genogram is a visual representation of the family tree, constructed by a family or family members, that focuses on the remembered emotional tone in the various relationships. The process of constructing the genogram serves many purposes. It shifts and defuses the interpersonal conflict by moving from the interpersonal to the intrapsychic; enables the central person to see his or her family of origin in a new light; and provides alternative explanations for current behavior. Moreover, as a result of these alternative explanations, the genogram helps other family members view the focal person differently.

The popularity of the genogram may be related to its utility in a wide variety of situations. For example, the genogram is used as a form of history gathering by most family therapists, regardless of their theoretical orientation. When completed, it provides an excellent database to be drawn on during the course of couple or family therapy. It is even used as an explanatory framework by many organizational consultants. McGoldrick and Gerson consider the genogram to be primarily an assessment tool (19), We, however, think of it as an intervention tool, since the entire family gets involved in collecting information and talking about the genogram—which results in a new and different understanding of each and every person in the relationship system.

Circular Questioning

A staple for relationship therapists in the early phase of treatment is *circular questioning,* an intervention technique developed by Selvini-Palazzoli (20) and enlarged and expanded on by others (21, 22). Selvini-Palazzoli refers to this most interesting technique as "the capacity of a therapist to conduct his investigation on the basis of feedback from the family in response to the information he solicits about relationships and, therefore, about difference and change" (20, p. 3). In this statement Selvini-Palazzoli makes clear that the intent of this type of interviewing is to ask questions about differences or changes rather than about the details of the events. With this form of questioning the therapist learns about the sequences and uses the feedback the family provides to set up the next question.

Role Playing and Family Sculpting

Role playing and family sculpting are most frequently used when the goal is to change the here-and-now interactional patterns and to actually begin this change during the session itself. Alone, these interventions are rarely powerful enough to provide lasting change. But when combined with structural, strategic, or individual therapy, they become the basis for significant second-order change.

In the symbolic-experiential techniques, of which these interventions are part, the goal is to provide the family with a completely new way to interact. The process of being involved in this new, therapist-choreographed interaction effectively helps families or couples to directly experience a new set of behaviors. Although only a few of the studies examining the efficacy of these therapies and techniques have demonstrated that they make a positive difference, it is noteworthy that frequently a family or couple remembers these exercises as the most powerful part of the therapy and attributes successful changes to the experiences.

Role playing and family sculpting both arose from psychodrama. *Role playing* is most easily done with dyads. The participants may be marital partners, but they can readily be parent/child or siblings. The goals are similar to those in the communication techniques: to initiate important new interactions and to change either unproductive or counterproductive interactions. Additional reasons for using this technique group are to promote awareness of the other person and to resolve the cognitive dissonance that often corrupts relationships.

Family sculpting takes role playing to another level. It is particularly valuable when young children are present; this is because the metaphors are the symbols rather than the words.

In one family a 7-year-old, chosen by the therapist to be the "conductor," was asked to pretend his family was made of clay and to mold their bodies into positions that represented how he experienced them. With some help, he positioned his mother with her head bowed, his younger sister on her knees clinging to her mother's leg, his father standing on a chair pointing his finger at his mother, and himself cowering in a corner. In this clear and concrete way he articulated his experience so that it was immediately understood by everyone in the family.

Appropriate questions following this exercise are: Who is closer to whom and by how much? What are the relationships among the participants? What posture is most characteristic of each person? What is a typical facial expression for each person? The list of possible variations of this exercise is almost endless.

Satir refined family sculpting to the point of developing four primary life positions. According to Satir's schema, a person can be a super-reasonable individual, a placater, a blamer, or a distractor (23). She would pantomime these and ask the conductor to use one of the four with each person he or she was sculpting. Once the tableau is completed, each person may be given a chance to express his or her feelings about the conductor's perception. In this way the conductor's viewpoint is acknowledged, even if not agreed with. At another point, family members may have the opportunity to create the picture that best shows how they would want the family to function. The therapy will then be directed to achieve the desired outcome.

Family sculpting is an important technique and is especially useful in work with larger groups. The technique involves physical activity rather than sitting and talking. The information derived from the exercise is personal and unambiguous to each participant, and the interpretations are not subject to reinterpretation. Family sculpting exercises typically are initiated when it appears that a visual metaphor will best clarify the patterns of relationships—including the boundaries, alliances, and coalitions within the family.

Environmental Interventions

Interventions with the larger ecosystem have also become an important part of relationship therapy. In a plan to help the family or the identified patient, therapists bring in people from the family's network or, alternatively, meet with people from the network (24).

Homework

Homework is another useful direct-intervention tactic. Like many of the intervention techniques previously mentioned, homework is a central element in the behavioral strategies. The content of the assignment—such as counting occurrences of an event and/or giving positive reinforcement (through, e.g., praise, tokens, or time spent with the person)—is less important to the outcome than both the process of doing the assignment and the structure of the assignment. For example, a couple who are fighting about the best way to discipline a child are told to count how often each of them positively reinforces the child. When they follow the directives of this assignment, the relationship between the couple, at least for the brief period, changes. During this time, too, the relationships within the family also change.

One can assign homework for many different reasons (25):

- To learn more about what happens between sessions
- To learn who participates in family endeavors and who does not
- To create a bridge between sessions
- To give more responsibility to patients
- To reinforce some important point made during therapy
- To change the interaction pattern outside the therapy setting

The key points for a therapist to remember when giving a homework assignment are outlined in Table 3–10.

Indirect-Intervention Approaches

Indirect intervention is used to circumvent the resistance of individuals and, most important, of the relationship system itself. These techniques assume reluctance and noncompliance and are directed to getting rid of or going around the barriers to change. The classic example, regularly repeated in the early family therapy literature, involves a child with school phobia. After several days

TABLE 3–10. **Assigning homework**

Frame the assignment positively.

Keep the assignment simple.

Define the desired behaviors clearly and concretely.

Give everyone a role in the assignment.

Always follow through to find out what happened.

of the child's refusal to go to school, as the story goes, the distraught mother brings the child to the therapist, only to find that there is no clear reason for the child's refusal. The therapist postulates that the problem resides in the mother-child bond, with both parties having difficulty separating. Rather than addressing the nature of the bond directly, the therapist, using an indirect approach, asks the father to take the child to school on a daily basis until the child is settled, thus circumventing the hypothesized relational problem, the mother-child bond.

In real life, therapeutic solutions are rarely as simple as this, but the idea is the same: identify the problem, consider the previous attempts to solve the problem, and design an intervention that circumvents the family's usual problem-solving techniques. Indirect interventions can be extremely effective when they also address, as in the school phobia story above, the relationships involved.

Paradox

One example of an indirect approach is the use of *paradox*. This technique is based on important linguistic principles (26) that make the technique seem more complicated than it really is. When people have to do things that are difficult for them, their natural instinct seems to be to keep doing what they've already been doing, only with more resolve. If the relationship therapist can help them stand back and see what they have to do from a different perspective, they often are able to succeed with ease.

Case Example

Jake, a 14-year-old with a conduct disorder, was in continual conflict with his authoritarian father. At the time of this intervention Jake had been in residential treatment for 6 months. During a family visit, Jake accused his father, Tom, of being abusive. Tom became enraged and for weeks was unable to think or speak of anything else during their sessions together.

He tried in every way he could think of to convince his son that he was not abusive. The harder he tried, the more entrenched Jake became. When it was suggested to Tom that abuse was a code word used in Jake's current treatment program, a subtle shift in attitude occurred. Tom wrote to Jake, inviting him to be open with his complaints and asking only that he not use the word "abuse." With permission to openly voice his objections to his father's behavior, Jake readily complied with the wish to change the language, and at last the relationship between father and son was able to progress.

Tom, with help, directed Jake to do what he had already been doing—complaining loudly and bitterly. In doing so, he was able to encourage a behavior that he previously could not tolerate. Jake took the opportunity to say things he previously had held in, until finally his anger lost its power and the two were able to talk about change.

Like reframing and positive connotation, described below, the introduction of paradox changes the mind-set of the entire family simultaneously in such a way that they can no longer see things the way they did in the past. When the family sees things differently, the relationships are necessarily changed, and individuals are freed from the confines of a dysfunctional system—one of the goals of interventions.

Common Understanding Techniques

Before the therapeutic plan can be implemented, the relationship therapist, as discussed earlier in the subsection on contracts, must be able to help the couple or family develop a common under-standing of the problem and a shared vision of the therapeutic direction. The techniques most commonly used to help develop a common understanding and a shared vision are reframing, posi-tive connotation, and metaphor. These three techniques all share the idea that since we frame our own reality, the clash of different ways of seeing things is what causes dissonance in relationships.

In addition, the stories we tell ourselves about ourselves, others, and the world become the frame of reference that determines our actions and interactions.

Reframing. Reframing is the most widely used technique to develop common understanding. The accuracy and precision of the therapist's interpretation or understanding is not as important as how the therapist articulates the interpretation. The interpretation should be both close enough to and significantly different from each individual's perceptions to allow them to both "buy into" and accept the reframing as a new and different explanation for the events and sequences. In some families many different perceptions and understandings must be taken into consideration.

Often therapists make the mistake of believing that reframing is sufficient to facilitate major change. Not so. Reframing the meaning of events in a relationship, whether done with an individual, a couple, or a family, is only the beginning.

Case Example

In one session an adult son, Joe, was trying to establish a relationship with his mother after several years of distance. The original "frame," or understanding, of the people present had three facets: Joe was distant because his wife and mother couldn't get along (mother's perception); Joe was distant because of religious differences (stepfather's perception); and Joe was distant because he was trying to establish his independence (Joe's perception). After the therapist inquired into the history of the family, both mother and son discussed the accidental death of Joe's biological father when Joe was 5 years old. Based on the intensity of his mother's affective response to this discussion, a new frame was proposed: mother and son had created and maintained distance to protect each other from the pain of that loss. This "reframing" paved the way for the essential work of a long-postponed grieving.

Positive connotation.   Positive connotation is a special form of reframing in which each person's behavior is redefined as being helpful or in the family's best interests. Positive connotation not only puts people on the same plane but also assumes and treats them as having a common interest—helping the family and each other. Furthermore, it avoids the problem that occurs when a singled-out individual misinterprets the intent, feels hurt, and becomes defensive.

Metaphor.   Metaphor, another form of reframing, makes use of the power of stories and myths to inform and guide human behavior. As a technique, metaphor draws on this power and can be used as a tool to redirect the family and the family's focus. Simply put, metaphor, as practiced by Erickson and his followers, is a form of indirectly giving directives by embedding them in stories and parables or within other instructions (27).

Storytelling is used specifically by the postmodern therapist, and generally by all of us. This technique, an essential part of RRT (see next chapter), is based on therapeutic understanding through dialogue. In storytelling the emphasis is on understanding current meaning. Past experiences are seen in the stories created in the present, and therapy becomes the process of shifting the patient's current problematic interactions with self and others to another set of stories that allows for a broader range of updated possibilities.

Prototypically, the postmodern therapist "deconstructs" the patient's story using a technique called *externalization*. Externalization is defined as "the linguistic separation of the problem from the personal identity of the patient" (28, p. 24). In effect, the postmodern therapist does not say, "You have a problem"; instead, he or she says, "Your problem is your enemy." Although this linguistic separation may seem like "all smoke and mirrors," the separation makes it easier for the patient to create a new story about the problem and finally to integrate that new story into his or her current life.

Several benefits occur when the entire family participates in the process of creating a new story that incorporates the facts that are known as well as the explanations for what is not known. Everyone is in the whole story together, and much of the anxiety of the unknown is resolved. Creating a new story is done through a multi-step process (29), such as outlined in Table 3–11.

■ GUIDELINE 8: ACQUIRE AND ORGANIZE DATA ABOUT THE INDIVIDUAL

At any point in the relationship therapy process, the therapist has the option either to continue to intervene in the system or to work directly with the individuals who make up the system. Many factors enter into making this choice or judgment call. The most important one is *timing,* which relates to the issues of safety and the availability of individuals to change; to the length of the therapeutic contact and contract; and to where the relationship is within the process of completing the contract.

Acquiring information about individuals in relationships is done indirectly through working with the system and discovering the reflections of the past in the present systemic interactions. Or it is done directly through inquiry into the situations and circumstances of the individuals' pasts—again in the context of the current here-and-now relational dynamics.

TABLE 3–11. **Creating a new story**

Find an acceptable name for the problem, such as fear, etc.

Make the problem, rather than a person, the problem.

Obtain a detailed history of the impact of the problem.

Determine when the problem has not dominated and build on this strength.

Gather many examples of success to support this viewpoint.

Plan for a future using this prospect.

Make the new perspective vivid by telling the new story in as many ways as possible.

Source. Adapted from O'Hanlon (29).

Let's use a brief vignette to clarify this essential point: in relationship therapy, work with an individual is most useful when it derives from, and is driven by, the here-and-now relational dynamics.

Case Example

Bob and Mildred were arguing in the office. During this argument Bob appeared to freeze; he got quiet, his eyes glazed over, and his body was still. However, Mildred went on without recognizing Bob's reaction, and as she continued her voice got louder and louder.

THERAPIST: Bob, what's going on?
(*Bob does not respond.*)
THERAPIST: Bob, you look as if you are frozen.
BOB (*nods agreement*)
THERAPIST: Is feeling frozen a familiar experience?
BOB: Yes, I get this way whenever we fight.
THERAPIST: Was this the same for you when you were growing up?
BOB: I think so. My mother and father fought all the time.
THERAPIST: As a child, what did you feel and do when they would fight?
BOB: I was terrified, and I would try to fade away.

With this sequence we have the basic information, the building blocks for the individual work. The here-and-now data—the reflections of the past in the present, Bob's response to the argument—were tracked to an early experience. Similar interventions could have been made with Mildred.

In relationship therapy any number of techniques can be used to acquire data about individuals and their early experiences. How the data are organized—how the therapist understands these elements—is, of course, highly dependent on the therapist's theoretical orientation.

■ GUIDELINE 9: MAKE INDIVIDUAL CHANGES

Strategies and techniques to facilitate individual change will be discussed in more detail in the next chapter. In brief, the process of individual change in the relationship context is similar to the process of change in individual therapy with one important difference. In individual therapy the starting point is either whatever the patient wants it to be or, in later stages of therapy, the transference relationship. In relationship therapy the starting point is the current interpersonal process.

Behavior therapists will use a number of techniques to facilitate individual change: relaxation, rehearsal, education, reinforcement, exposure, flooding, and so forth. The work will be present oriented. Insight-oriented therapists may or may not track the affect, and they use support, clarification, and interpretation as the primary tools. The individual work can be present oriented or historical. Again, the important element is the reference point. In individual therapy it is the individual patient; in relationship therapy the starting point for exploring individual issues is the interpersonal process.

It is also important to remember that not everyone in a family will or needs to do individual work for the therapy to be successful (30). In fact, whether or not a family or a family member does any individual work depends on the circumstances, the resources (time and money), and the relevance of the individual changes to the current circumstances. One does not have to be perfect—only good enough.

■ GUIDELINE 10: CREATE NEW AND HEALTHY RELATIONSHIP SYSTEMS

New and healthy relationships don't just happen as a consequence of therapy. People who enter adulthood without having learned the basic skills to conduct themselves, to manage their emotions, and to be active participants in a relationship will need to learn these skills after the emotional impediments to learning have been removed.

A vision for the future is developed once the blocks to learning are removed. The components and prerequisites to fulfilling this vision are then flushed out, the essential skills are clarified, new behaviors are rehearsed, and, finally, future challenges are anticipated, and responses to those challenges are planned.

There are many ways to teach the skills of healthy relationships. One way is to provide patients with concrete rules for keeping relationships healthy (Table 3–12). These rules have already proved useful in business and management (31), and we apply them to families and couples as well.

No secrets.   Secrets, by definition, exist without the knowledge of others. Designed for escaping notice or observation, they undermine trust and teamwork in the relationship. Secrets promote doubt, suspiciousness, and even a feeling of being crazy. They lead to affairs and other deviancies that injure the health of the relationship and the individuals affected by them.

No surprises.   Because of their unexpectedness and strangeness, unpleasant surprises can shock others, thereby undermining the intimacy and predictability of a relationship.

No lies.   Lies are false statements made in the deliberate intent to deceive. When parents lie, kids also lie. And when partners lie,

---

TABLE 3–12.   **Rules for healthy relationships**

No secrets

No surprises

No lies

No distractions

No excuses

No illusions

Source.   Adapted from Rodgers et al. (31).

there is no chance of really knowing each other, so intimacy is perpetually undermined. When there are lies. there are problems in the relationship, whatever the relationship is.

No distractions.   Distractions divide attention, prevent concentration, and interfere with problem solving. Distractions are what dysfunctional systems are made of. They undermine the competencies of individuals, prevent opportunities to learn and grow, destroy the predictability of the relationship, and inhibit intimacy.

No excuses.   Excuses are pleas offered as a reason for being pardoned or exempted from responsibility. Self-justifications that are in fact rationalizations, they undermine taking individual responsibility for one's actions and the impact of behavior on others in the relationship system.

No illusions.   Illusions deceive by producing a false impression. Healthy relationships accept and deal with what is real, whether that is a child's learning problem or a partner's substance abuse or physical disability.

When families and couples follow these six rules, they are less vulnerable to both the normal and the unexpected adversities of today's life. They are more able to develop the specific skills, social competencies, and attitudes that help them to handle stress and avoid self-destructive behavior.

Fortunately, the relationship therapist is also able to turn to a set of research-based criteria that aid in teaching people to create new and healthy relationship systems (9). Our rendition of the elements of healthy relationship systems is presented in Table 3–13.

Relationships are all different because people are all different. Therefore, the problems that families and couples bring to therapy are all different. However, the steps and rules for keeping relationships healthy are the same—and they work.

TABLE 3–13. **Healthy relationship systems**

Problems are identified early and solved quickly in a caring and direct way.

People stay active and involved with each other.

Cooperation, working together, and team learning are encouraged.

Individual interests and achievements are supported.

Caring behaviors and appreciations are shown openly.

Change is accepted, and people are committed to making change happen.

A sense of fun, interest, and excitement is present.

The short- and long-term focuses are positive.

People are more important than things.

■ REFERENCES

1. Senge P: The Fifth Discipline: The Art and Practice of the Learning Organization. New York, Doubleday, 1990

2. Prochaska J, DiClemente C: Stages of change in the modification of problem behaviors. Prog Behav Modif 28:183–218, 1992

3. Smith D: Taking Charge of Change: Ten Principles for Managing People and Performance. New York, Addison-Wesley, 1996

4. Polster E, Polster M: Gestalt Therapy Integrated: Contours of Theory and Practice. New York, Vintage, 1974

5. Minuchin S, Montalvo B, Guerney B, et al: Families of the Slums: An Exploration of Their Structure and Treatment. New York, Basic Books, 1967

6. Pinsof W, Wynne LC: The efficacy of marital and family therapy: an empirical review and conclusion. Journal of Marital and Family Therapy 21:585–613, 1995

7. Group for the Advancement of Psychiatry, Committee on the Family: Global Assessment of Relational Functioning Scale (GARF): background and rationale. Fam Process 35:155–172, 1996

8. Global Assessment of Relational Functioning (GARF) Scale, in Diagnostic and Statistical Manual of Mental Disorders, 4th Edition (DSM-IV). Washington, DC, American Psychiatric Association, 1994, pp 758–759

9. Lewis J, Beavers R, Sosett J, et al: No Single Thread: Psychological Health in Family's Systems. New York, Brunner/Mazel, 1976

10. Gottman J, Levinson R: A valid procedure for obtaining self affect and marital interaction. J Consult Clin Psychol 53:151–60, 1985

11. Gottman J: Why Marriages Succeed or Fail. New York, Simon & Schuster, 1994

12. Andersen T: The reflecting team: dialogue and meta-dialogue in clinical work. Fam Process 26:415–428, 1987

13. Moos R, Moos B: Family Environment Scale Manual, Revised Edition. Palo Alto, CA, Consulting Psychologists Press, 1986

14. Olson D, Russell C, Speckle D: Circumplex Model: Systemic Assessment of Families, 2nd Edition. New York, Haworth, 1989

15. Epstein N, Baldwin L, Bishop D: The McMaster Family Assessment Device. Journal of Marital and Family Therapy 92:171–180, 1983

16. Miller I, Kabakoff R, Epstein N, et al: The development of a clinical rating scale for the McMaster Model of Family Functioning. Fam Process 33:53–70, 1994

17. McClendon R, Kadis L: A model of integrating individual and family therapy: the contract is the key, in Brief Therapy: Myths, Methods and Metaphors. Edited by Zeig J, Munion W. New York: Brunner/Mazel, 1990, pp 135–150

18. Selvini-Palazzoli M, Boscolo L, Cecchin G, et al: Paradox and Counterparadox: A New Model for Therapy in the Family in Schizophrenic Transition. New York, Jason Aronson, 1978

19. McGoldrick M, Gerson R: Genograms in Family Assessment. New York, WW Norton, 1985

20. Selvini-Palazzoli M, Boscolo L, Cecchin G, et al: Hypothesizing-Circularity-Neutrality: three guidelines for the conductor of the session. Fam Process 19:3–12, 1980

21. Tomm K: Interventive interviewing, Part III: intending to ask lineal, circular, strategic, or reflexive questions? Fam Process 27:1–15, 1988

22. Penn P: Circular questioning. Fam Process 21:267–280, 1982

23. Satir V: Peoplemaking. Palo Alto, CA, Science and Behavior Press, 1972

24. Speck R, Rueveni U: Network therapy: a developing concept. Fam Process 8:182–191, 1969

25. Budman S, Gurman AS: Theory and Practice of Brief Therapy. New York, Guilford, 1988

26. Watzlawick P, Weakland JH, Fisch R. Change: Principles of Problem Formation and Problem Resolution. New York, WW Norton, 1974

27. Zeig J: Seeding, in Brief Therapy: Myths, Methods and Metaphors. Edited by Zeig J, Munion W. New York: Brunner/Mazel, 1990, pp 221–246

28. White M, Epston D: Narrative Means to Therapeutic Ends. New York, WW Norton, 1990

29. O'Hanlon W: The third wave. Family Therapy Networker 18:18–26, 1994

30. Bader E: Redecisions in family therapy: a study of change in an intensive family workshop. Dissertation Abstracts No 7625064, 1976

31. Rodgers T, Taylor W, Foreman R: No Excuses Management: Proven Systems for Starting Fast, Growing Quickly, and Surviving Hard Times. New York, Doubleday, 1993

4

REDECISION
RELATIONSHIP THERAPY

Since the 1950s, when a few mental health practitioners became convinced of the enormous importance of the present as well as the past, marital and family therapists have sought an integrated theoretical base that simultaneously takes into account the history of individual members of the family, the history of the family unit, and the current interaction among family members. In the relationship therapy field today, several such theories have emerged that are both innovative and valuable in their contributions, thus allowing therapists various options for doing couple and family therapy within an integrated framework. Therapists can choose which theoretical or therapeutic approach best fits their own orientation as well as the treatment situation.

In the service of being concise, we have chosen in this chapter to outline and discuss in more complete detail one of the integrated models currently available for working with families and couples, Redecision Relationship Therapy (RRT), which we developed in the early 1970s and have used ever since. This model is presented to exemplify how one cohesive approach can delineate a focus, utilize contracts, combine systems thinking with individual work, supply insight, and elicit affect—all within a single unified structure. The model gives direction and structure to the marital or family treatment process, allows for many forms of psychotherapeutic intervention, and permits these interventions to be suitably determined by the situation of the relationship. RRT can be used in many different therapeutic structures, from long-term treatment or intensive multiple-family groups to brief, time-limited, and even single-session interventions.

■ ORIGINS AND EVOLUTION OF REDECISION THERAPY

Redecision therapy was developed by Robert and Mary Goulding over 30 years ago (1, 2). The underlying concept of redecision therapy is that each child has the power to make unique choices about himself or herself—about how to think, feel, and be in the world. Over time and through the constant repetition of the parent-child-family interaction, these choices become what are called *early decisions.* Redecisions are cognitive and affective reinterpretations of the early childhood decisions or beliefs about the self.

To be more specific, the young child's inner needs and the intensity with which they are experienced; the availability of the parents and family to respond to the child, along with the quality and consistency (or unpredictability) of this response; and the time period over which the responses are made—all of these factors create the environment to which a child must adapt. At the most basic level, the child must adapt to this environment in order to survive; at the next level, to feel the least pain; and at the highest level, to feel actual pleasure. Through this process of adapting, individuals build an internal model of the self that is based on relationships with parents or parenting persons and, later, with people in the outside world. This early established model is then carried by each person throughout life—into every room, every experience, and every relationship.

This theory of early decisions and early decision making is closely akin to many other current theories based on the idea of the creation of core beliefs about the self and others. According to many of the cognitive therapies, for instance, core beliefs act as a template for the perception of the rest of life's decisions and interactions. So, too, do early decisions serve as templates.

Redecisions are revised beliefs about the self. The redecision occurs with the here-and-now incorporation of updated and current information about one's self and circumstances. Through the redecision process, individuals take steps to free themselves to think, feel, and behave differently in their current lives—to make free choices in the present rather than to react with the resounding echoes of the past.

■ RELATIONSHIP THERAPY AND REDECISIONS

When two or more people come together for any period of time, they form a relationship unit. Depending on the length of time they are together, the commonality of their interests (through work, friendship, or kinship, for instance), and the strength of their bond, each unit or system develops a specific character of its own.

The system has its own process, or way of functioning. It also has a structure and a set of rules that define its day-to-day operating style. A basic understanding of how the relationship system works is shared, although not usually articulated, by the members of the couple or family. This shared understanding can provide comfort and a sense of inclusion and belonging, plus the safety that allows its members to grow and to begin exploring themselves and the outside world. Or it can be detrimental to all or some of its members. When the shared understanding is detrimental, it is the power of the early decisions, plus a rigid adherence to the corresponding response patterns of other system members, that creates the relationship problem.

In the early to mid-1970s we created the Redecision Family Therapy Model by adding the ideas of systems theory to the basic concepts of redecision therapy with individuals. We first developed the three-stage model for working with relationships after observing that current behavior in the form of interactional patterns, and personal history in the form of early decisions, operate in a reciprocal relationship. Over the years the model has been refined and expanded to incorporate all relationship forms, not just family therapy.

RRT is an integrative approach that

- Appreciates the mutual power and importance of both the individual and system dynamics.
- Recognizes the interface of both the past and the present in the context of current difficulties.
- Honors the overlap of the present and the future.
- Respects the contributions of the different schools of psychotherapy.
- Recognizes the need for an integrative framework for the application of many different theoretical principles and therapeutic techniques.

RRT incorporates the ideas of early decisions into relationship systems. We postulate that when children become adults, they choose marital and life partners whose early models of themselves and the world interface with their own in a way that not only allows but actually encourages the continuation of early beliefs or decisions. Partner A's model will, in fact, provide evidence that Partner B's internal model is correct and therefore should be maintained. In other words, when selecting a partner, a person tries to make life as predictable and secure as possible by choosing someone whose background, style, and early decisions will allow for the patterns of interaction to reinforce his or her early decisions. In this way the past and the present always interface.

Furthermore, when parents are raising a family, the messages given to children about how to think, feel, and be are also congruent with the parents' early decisions—and therefore aimed toward making life predictable for the parents. In fact, much of people's daily interaction is a continual negotiation to obtain a measure of congruence between their inner experience and their perceived reality. The patterns of interaction to be seen in the system are consequently the net result of each person's attempt to negotiate the difference between inner and outer realities and between the perceptions of self and others. It is predictable that when the patterns are limited in number, shallow in depth, and rigidly adhered to, the relationship will suffer and some of its members will experience psychological and/or physical distress.

Redecision Relationship Therapy is a method of changing the dysfunctional patterns of interaction in relationships. By helping individuals incorporate updated and current information into their early childhood models of themselves and their world, they are able to create new and healthy relationship systems. This process is much like weaving. Individuals learn that they had, and indeed still have, the power and the responsibility to weave the fabric of their own lives. They are taught how the threads of the past and the present intertwine; that each person had woven their own fabric the first time as children; and that, most important, as adults now, they can reweave the fabric of their lives and their relationships as they choose.

Each redecision signals a step in transforming the self. Each redecision opens up the opportunity for new and different systems interactions, as well as the opportunity for other family system members to move ahead with their own growth process.

■ **PROFILING THE MODEL:**
   AN OVERVIEW

Redecision Relationship Therapy is a three-stage model that integrates systems theory, transactional analysis, and gestalt and psychodrama techniques. The three stages are presented as a linear progression. However, in real life the process is more of a shifting entity that flexibly accommodates relationships and circumstances as they really are. As with any form of therapy, both the presenting circumstances and the depth of the pathology drive the model. A brief journey through the model is shown in Figure 4–1.

Although we describe the three stages of the model as distinct entities, as noted above, they are rarely clearly demarcated. For example, while a family is involved directly in the work of one stage, the work on other stages may be going on as well. Movement back and forth among the three stages is continual. A progression through the stages can occur within one interview and does occur throughout the entire treatment process. Research on the model has proven that doing the intrapsychic work of the second stage is not necessary for each individual in the relationship. Therefore, in many instances couples and families proceed from Stage I to Stage III without actually doing the individual work of Stage II. This is one of the advantages of an integrated model; it flexibly meets the needs of the individuals and the relationship.

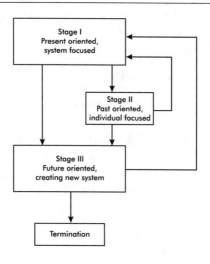

FIGURE 4–1.   **The Redecision Relationship Therapy model.**

Stage I: Systems

In the first stage of RRT, the *systems* stage, the focus is on symptom or problem resolution through changes in both the structure and the function of the system. The purpose of this initial stage is emancipation of the individual from the emotional tangle and problems that dominate the relationship. Stage I examines, and then interrupts, the ongoing and continuous interactional patterns that negatively affect problem-solving behavior, positive coping skills, task mastery, social competence, and intimacy. The interface of defenses, mental models, or early decisions, and how they manifest themselves in the present, are defined in Stage I.

Stage II: Individual

In the second stage of RRT, the *individual* (or intrapersonal or intrapsychic) *stage,* the main focus shifts to the transformation of internal models. This involves helping the individual confront his or her past, to gain the confidence to master the present and decide on the future. The focal point for changing internal models or making redecisions is derived from each individual's own process and participation with other system members.

Stage III: Reintegration

In the third stage of RRT, the *reintegration stage,* the focus is on prevention of future disablement, both individual and systemic, through teaching of new effective and healthy ways to function within the interpersonal system. Psychoeducational and specific behavioral interventions that provide information and teach new skills are particularly valuable in Stage III, when the emotional temperature has been lowered.

Now, having generally outlined the three stages of RRT, we will detail how they are utilized in designing and conducting a therapeutic approach to working with couples and families.

■ APPLYING THE MODEL

The first challenge for the therapist utilizing RRT is the same as for any therapist regardless of the model being used—individual or relationship, insight oriented or behaviorally focused. The challenge is to create a safe environment in which relationship members will reveal themselves in their natural state. Creating such an environment is a crucial but sometimes daunting task, since families and couples usually restrict or distort their behaviors, thoughts, and feelings when in the presence of outsiders. We particularly stress the importance of establishing an environmental structure within the therapy room that is safe and confidential—one in which people are allowed to move, act, and be whoever they really are.

Within this protected environment we are able to observe, with some degree of accuracy, how the family operates as a whole, as well as each individual's readiness level for change within the relationship unit. We begin our contact at the level that will be both acceptable to and viewed as supportive of the family or couple. We quickly seek ways to discern and then emphasize the strengths and resources of both the relationship and the individuals involved in it. The overall flow of therapy is guided by the principles outlined in Table 4–1.

Stage I: Systems

In utilizing RRT, we incorporate all of the guidelines for doing relationship therapy that were presented in Chapter 3. We are solidly

---

TABLE 4–1. **Guiding principles of Redecision Relationship Therapy**

Know where you are going and keep it positive.

Focus on current interactions and how they impede relationship health.

Help each person learn how his or her behavior impacts others.

Motivate people to take responsibility for their own decisions and change.

Move toward creating new and healthy relationship dynamics.

---

based in an integrated theoretical approach (Guideline 1). Our commitment is to working with the relationship, and we are always *thinking family* (Guideline 2). We understand the change process (Guideline 3) and the importance of making contact within the relationship's own frame of reference (Guideline 4).

In the systems stage of RRT (Guideline 5), interventions serve the purpose of reinforcing individual boundaries, interrupting maladaptive patterns of interaction, and both defining and supporting the establishment of new interactional patterns. Specifically, the process is one of assessing and intervening in the here-and-now interactions, with the intention of perceiving various reflections of the early decision within the present. These reflections are discovered through picking up the verbal and nonverbal indications of the early decision and working through the defensive reaction to the core beliefs. The therapeutic tasks of Stage I are summarized in Table 4–2.

The goal of Stage I is to free the individual from the system and help him or her become available, in Stage II, to discover the significance of the early decision and work through the now outdated early belief to redecision. Stage I starts with the first patient contact (Guideline 4) and continues through acquiring and organizing systems data (Guideline 5), forming therapeutic contracts (Guideline 6), and making systems interventions (Guideline 7). Stage I concludes as individuals are freed enough from the dysfunctional system dynamics to safely inquire into themselves.

TABLE 4–2. **Redecision Relationship Therapy:**
            Stage I therapy tasks

Create a safe environment.

Assess readiness.

Acquire and organize systems information.

Form contracts.

Separate the individual from the system.

Educate.

Model.

In assessing the relationship, we watch the flow of information, the impediments to that flow, what happens to the expression of affect, how disagreements are handled, and a host of similar variables. In other words, we note the order and sequence of events that occur in interviews. We also note what does not occur that might be expected to. Since each relationship has a unique way of functioning, with a uniquely characteristic pattern of information flow and expression of affect, we observe and note the recurrence of these patterns.

Furthermore, we look at the structure of the family or couple relationship. We are interested in the hierarchy of the relationship and the alliances and coalitions that have developed. We use the concept of *boundaries* and concern ourselves with three different boundary configurations (3).

The first boundary configuration, the *internal minor* (or *self*) *boundary,* comprises the set of characteristics by which individuals distinguish themselves from each other. When this boundary is absent, people are not able to separate what is inside them from what is outside, nor can they distinguish what is real from what is not real. An accompanying rigidity of this boundary, on the other hand, excludes any significant or close contact with others.

The second configuration of concern, the *internal major boundary,* separates leadership from nonleadership. Without clear and congruent leadership, day-to-day life becomes chaotic. In today's healthy relationships, leadership is exercised by all relationship members, whether simultaneously or by turns. Although active leadership varies at different times and with different situations, equal partners work together to set goals and make decisions. In healthy families, a good idea is acted on and implemented—regardless of who originated or proposed it. Relationship checks and balances operate to keep tasks on track and therefore to avoid costly errors.

The third configuration, the *external boundary,* comprises the set of characteristics by which the family unit knows itself. This boundary is defined by the values that guide the behaviors of individuals within the family and of the family as a unit.

The tools used to make the systems assessment are any of those defined in the previous chapter. Primarily we are active therapists and therefore use the direct-observation techniques, such as the numerous structured tasks.

Clearly defined goals and working agreements that focus on resolving the underlying interpersonal and dynamic difficulties are an essential part of our work (Guideline 6). Contracts facilitate the psychotherapeutic process by providing a goal-oriented structure that defines all deviations as a form of avoidance of solving the relationship problems. In other words, contracts serve both as a focal point for the work of psychotherapy and as a reference point for digressions.

As therapists, we initially consider how the structure and process of the family or couple relationship either help or hinder resolution of the problem. We then consider the individual pain and struggles associated with the presenting problem.

Next, we—therapist and patients together—are ready to mutually develop the contract. In effect, the contract says,

> If you as a couple or family change in these specific ways, you will have the best chance of resolving your problem. Furthermore, as individuals you have each struggled with the problem in your own characteristic way. If you resolve the individual core problem—if you change the model of yourself and the world that you carry around inside—you will eliminate your personal pain, plus allow yourself and the other persons involved in the problem the best opportunity to prevent similar difficulties and situations from occurring in the future.

The following case outlines the importance of contracts and how they fit into the flow of relationship therapy.

Case Example

Susan, a 47-year-old married woman, was referred to us after her fourth conviction for shoplifting. She had served time following previous convictions and was currently facing the possibility of being "put away" for an extended period. In the past Susan had received extensive individual therapy. This time her astute lawyer realized that the individual therapy had been unsuccessful and referred her for marital therapy as well. The judge in her case eventually granted an extended probationary status, community service, and continued long-term relationship and individual therapy in lieu of jail time.

When we first saw Bill and Susan, they had been married for 18 years. Their two children were in college and doing well. There were many strains in their life together, but money was not an issue and never had been. Upon examination, Susan's early life and personal history revealed no unusual or traumatic events. In fact, Susan could be said to have come from a "normal family." The second of three children, she was raised in the Midwest by both parents. After completing 2 years of college, she was successfully employed before marriage.

The atmosphere in the room when Bill and Susan were there could best be described as somewhere between chaos and pandemonium. Susan was vocal and explosive, but also vague and inconsistent. She had no apparent insight about the cause of her shoplifting or the antecedents of her behavior. Moreover, she was not able to focus on her actions for more than one sentence before she would be off on another tangent—invariably complaining about her husband. It was as if her own actions were completely alien to her and, as such, she dismissed them. She complained that Bill "is always on my case," and considered him critical and jealous, and also untrustworthy with respect to the family finances.

Bill's response to Susan's outbursts was to look down. One had the feeling that if Bill could physically disappear, he would. He, too, had little insight into his wife's behavior. In fact, he knew so little about it that he learned only a week before she was due in court that she had been arrested again.

Bill and Susan were seen as enmeshed and relatively undifferentiated—and, as a result, unable to accept adult responsibilities.

Within several sessions, Bill and Susan agreed that their mutual dependency prevented them from noticing, commenting on, and correcting problems. The contract that Bill and Susan agreed to obligated both of them to become more self-reliant, self-assured, and independent so that they could develop more functional and mature ways of helping each other.

Within couple therapy, Bill was able to acknowledge the serious flaws in his way of managing stress and his life in general. For the first time, he saw his own failure to notice anything or anyone outside of himself—including his wife. His personal difficulties, along with his attempts to manage them, were seen as a result of his early decision that he was basically a bumbling, incompetent idiot. Bill's individual contract was to open his eyes and discover who he really was, rather than to go on blindly believing what his father and brothers had told him when he was growing up.

Susan recognized and agreed that as much as she loved and cared for Bill, her way of helping him—becoming a little girl and shoplifting so that he could focus on her and not have to deal with his internal stress—was definitely not working. Moreover, she also recognized that her behavior derived from her early decision to never grow up. She quickly figured out that when she acted like a little girl, with temper tantrums and no limits or respect for others, she effectively had stopped all grown-up thinking. Susan formulated her individual contract: to "grow up" and honor herself as a competent, responsible, and gracious woman. She knew that when she could do this, she would no longer act out by shoplifting.

After contracts are agreed on, the therapist, working closely with the family, designs and executes interventions that will change personal and interpersonal boundaries, the structure of the family, and the patterns of interaction (Guideline 7).

As an example of this process, let's consider the Baker family. Its main structural defect was that all of the family units (five brothers and sisters and their families) had been linked into one conglomerate, which was bound together through the relationship with Ray's mother, in whom the emotional power of the entire family resided.

Case Example

Carol and Ray came to see us as a referral from Ray's employee assistance program (EAP) at work. They were a couple in serious crisis. Carol was about to leave the marriage and move elsewhere. Ray's mother, Mary, informed of this, had already filed charges against Carol for the anticipated removal of her grandchildren. Mary was urging her son to file at once for divorce and full custody and, in fact, had already paid the full legal retainer.

In the first session we heard Carol's not unreasonable objection to how Ray's mother, on a weekly basis for the 6 years of their marriage, had collected Ray's paycheck (even though he was 42 years old). This reigning matriarch would bank his money, walk next door to where they lived, and then give cash to Ray and Carol, along with her detailed instructions as to how to spend it during the coming week. Whenever Carol objected to this practice, Ray would loyally defend his mother, saying that she still did this for all her five children, each of whom was grown and competently employed. "Why should it be any different for you and me?" Ray would scream at Carol.

We confronted the dynamics of this extremely enmeshed family, including the various control tactics and guilt games that inhibited Ray and Carol from forming a separate and cohesive subunit with their children. We used games, genograms, and drawings to help Ray view his mother in a different light and to encourage both Ray and Carol to be able to voice whatever discomfort they felt about their situation.

The overall contract for the Ray and Carol Baker family was to establish themselves as an autonomous family unit with an individual life of their own. Through this contract and direct instructions, Carol was able to curtail her attacks on Mary, and this provided relief to Ray from perpetually having to defend his mother. He was then freed up to see and react in new ways to his mother's controlling nature, in which all her children had cooperated (including all their spouses except for Carol). Once the boundaries were established around the unit of Carol, Ray, and their children, they proceeded with their life together in a new and healthy way.

Numerous intervention options are possible during the first stage. They may be direct or indirect, fast or slow, light or heavy. We choose different combinations to constantly maintain a balance between confrontation and support. This balance provides safety and facilitates progress.

The following is a dialogue from work with Brenda and John, in which Brenda is explaining in her words how the interactions with John got in the way of their relationship and how they affect her personally. This is a good example of how RRT is applied, illustrating our thinking and responses as we work with relationships.

RUTH: Do you have any idea what happens when things go wrong between you?

BRENDA: I think it is the little things that I don't know how to resolve with him that get us into trouble.

RUTH: For example?

BRENDA: Well . . . Like I walk in the door, and John is there to always comment on how I look. I seem to have grown up without learning how to dress myself. But it's much more than that, because I have to dress according to what's acceptable to John. I could dress fine and be all happy with how I look. But I try to make it happy and fine with John because I have to walk down the street with him.

RUTH: Will you say more?

BRENDA: Okay, I walk through the door, and I'm all happy. I have a new outfit on, and while I'm at work everybody tells me how nice I look. But then I walk in the door, and John says, "Oh my God, you wore that sweater with those shoes!" . . . or something like that.

RUTH: And then what happens for you?

BRENDA: I just . . . my heart drops and I hurt because I'm thinking, What does he like about me anyway? He doesn't like my hair, he doesn't like my clothes, he is not crazy about my friends. I just carry it right on up and out and even wonder why I am here at all.

This was an opportunity, within the context of the system, to learn more about how Brenda operated as she interacted in the relationship or else to turn to John and investigate his part of the system. This is a typical choice point. How does the therapist continue with the systemic interaction? We chose in this instance to go with acquiring more information about how Brenda thought and felt about herself within the system.

RUTH: There you are, your heart drops and you begin to carry things up and out. What do you think and feel about yourself at this point?

BRENDA: What I honestly think about myself is . . . I question whether or not I am good enough for him. And how can I be better, and how can I deal with this?

RUTH: So you question your abilities to deal with John and whether he likes anything about you and if you are good enough for him?

BRENDA: Exactly. Yeah, I question myself, and that is what makes the distance between us.

This information about Brenda's internal process had been gathered from her participation in the system and from her understanding of how things worked between John and her. Here we could choose to further investigate Brenda's beliefs about herself; to continue in the here and now and gather more information about how Brenda operated in the system; or to make a bridge to work with John. Work with relationships is constantly full of such choices. Since this was only the second interview, we chose to return to learn more about Brenda in the system.

RUTH: Tell me more of what you mean when you say that this is what makes the distance between you and John.

BRENDA: I think what happens with me is that I hold a lot of things in. There are little things that aren't quite right.

You know, that I haven't quite followed through to bring up. This is just in the relationship. Issues that I haven't dealt with for one reason or another. And they build up, and then finally I get angry and I just yell and complain . . . and it all pours out, kind of like vomit. And then after that I am really scared. As a matter of fact, I did it the other night. I was incredibly depressed. I was more depressed than I can remember being in a long time, and I sat on the couch and then I just started and I threw it all up. I just started yelling all of it. Interestingly, John was different this time. He just listened. I was so scared and upset, but we finally talked about it.

Here Brenda offered the opportunity for us to begin the transition to the other part of the system: learning about how John operates in the relationship. Ruth accepted the invitation and began to switch the focus.

RUTH: So John was different, and it was helpful. What happens if John is going to blow it?

BRENDA: If he's going to blow it, he'll say that what I say isn't true and that he didn't do that. He'll come back at me angry and hard. That is really a perfect example, because when he does that I sink farther and farther away from him. After the other night when he wasn't contrary with me, I felt more accepted. I felt better after I shared all of that with him. And after he had taken it all in, then I could make love to him.

Now that we had begun to refocus and make the bridge to the other part of the system, more information was needed about the interactional patterns, so we turned to continue with John.

LES: What is your perception of this, John?

JOHN: For me, when she starts yelling I either explode or I slow down, and wonder how I have been with her, and then that is what gets me back in control. Slowing down and taking notice is what literally gets me back inside my body. I mean, I'm so mad that I've traveled. I have literally gone somewhere else on my insides, and yet I am still in that fight with her. And I know that in order to get straight with things, I have to settle up with myself. And then I can come back and tell myself and Brenda, "I did it" and "I'm sorry."

LES: Okay. So you need to come back to yourself and to take responsibility for what was your part?

JOHN: Uh huh.

By this point we learned more about the system and gathered information about what happened internally with each of the persons participating in the relationship. We arrived at this information from what was presented in the here-and-now system dynamics and from directly asking each individual about his or her internal process.

Individual patterns that occur over and over again within a couple's or family's interactions direct the therapist to a possible individual inquiry into the origins of the beliefs displayed in the interaction. In this sequence we were able to pick up through Brenda's verbal and nonverbal interactions the footprint of an early decision.

Somewhat later in the same interview, we initiated an inquiry into Brenda's family of origin and found that she had been raised by her mother and an abusive stepfather, who both verbally and physically attacked her any time she spoke up against him. Brenda had learned early on that keeping quiet was the safest and only way to get along. Her two younger half-sisters, the apples of her stepfather's eye, could do no wrong, whereas Brenda was constantly told by her stepfather that she wasn't good enough for the family.

Her reaction was always to look for ways to be better so she could measure up to whatever it was he wanted—and therefore be allowed to remain with her mother in this family.

Brenda's family-of-origin situation had constantly confronted her with the question of how she might deal with a cruel and dangerous situation in order to survive. She perceived that a similar question was being brought up again and again in her present-day situation with John. And, of course, John was in full cooperation with Brenda's early decision, which implied, in effect, "I'm not good enough, and so I must always try to change and be better." This early decision became the basis of Brenda's participation in the current relationship system and also John's interface with her.

Stage II: Individual

How is one's identity, one's self-concept, formed? As mentioned earlier, in redecision theory the building blocks for this internal model of the self are called *early decisions.* The child's step-by-step process of accommodation or adaptation to the world around him or her is called *early decision making.*

Redecisions are made when an individual's thinking, feeling, and being as a child are reexperienced and connected with adult competence, assets, and abilities. In the process of making redecisions, individuals metaphorically become the child of 3 or 7 or 10, while carrying the knowledge of the present, and of the person they are in the present, with them. With the structure and guidance provided by the therapist and using their own current strengths and abilities, persons are helped to regard themselves, the situation, and the other people in their lives differently. Through the redecision process individuals are freed from self-restricting early decisions that in a sense hold them captive, so that they can think, feel, and behave differently in the current relationship. The therapeutic tasks of Stage II are summarized in Table 4–3.

As mentioned earlier, parents and the world in which the child grows up are perceived as delivering messages to the child about how to think, feel, and behave. Many of these messages are caring and nurturing, instructive, and supportive. There are also, of course, constricting or negative messages. Called *injunctions,* these negative messages are framed as prohibitions, in the form of "don'ts." Some of these don'ts are Don't grow up; Don't think, feel, or succeed; Don't be a child; Don't be (alive); and Don't be you. Early decisions are made in response to the negative and constricting messages. The particular "don'ts" of each family are related to the parents' need to keep life predictable by supporting their own personal early decisions about themselves,

Until recently, redecision theory considered that the mechanism by which injunctions exert their potent influence lies in the power inherent in the parents and other significant caretakers. However, since affect theory has come to light, particularly the work of Nathanson (4) on shame affect, new opportunities to explore the development of early decisions and early decision making have arisen. Affect theory redefines the early decision-making concept, pointing out that it is the presence of affect that directs our attention to certain stimuli and that, accordingly, it is the absence of affect that allows each of us to ignore or discount stimuli.

We now postulate that when an infant or child, perhaps engaged in positive action that promotes his or her own development, receives a don't message, the message evokes shame affect, which has profound physiologic consequences. Thus, the young child has two tasks: he or she must learn to minimize the impact of shame affect in order to continue functioning and at the same time learn

---

TABLE 4–3. **Redecision Relationship Therapy: Stage II therapy tasks**

Help patients move from here and now to there and then.

Guide patients to discover their early decisions and understand their value.

Empower patients to make redecisions.

---

to avoid or minimize the painful parental or environmental consequences of the "don't" prohibitions.

With time and repetition, the child's defensive maneuvers against both shame affect and parental injunctions become ingrained and reified as early decisions. Like shame, early decisions affect one's view of oneself. They are experienced as if they were "me"; they are sometimes preverbal, and most usually operate far from awareness.

In summary, an early decision is now seen to be made in response to the combined impact of parental or other external input and shame affect. In other words, the internal force influencing early decision making is shame affect; the external force is the injunction/attribution process and the necessity to respond in some way. The early decision is the belief about the self that the child formulates that accommodates simultaneously the demands of the internal preprogramming and those of the environment in which the child is living. An early decision is a decision about how to manage—or, in some families, how to survive.

RRT's primary framework for recognizing and organizing individual data (Guideline 8) is built around the concept of early decisions. This process of early decision making is demonstrated in the following typical example of what is just a normal part of most families' lives.

Case Example

During a session with her mother, 3-year-old Kim was delightedly and delightfully pirouetting around the office, her dress swirling in the air and immodestly exposing her bare midriff and panties. She was completely oblivious to anything but the pleasure of showing off. Her mother's "Don't do that!" brought an instantaneous response during which she stopped dancing, her eyes turned away, her shoulders slumped, and her thumb went into her mouth. The experience was obviously not too traumatic but could have evoked memories of other "don'ts" in Kim's personal memory file.

The next time Kim came into the office, she acted much more reserved. Although it cannot be definitely declared that Kim had made an early decision at this point, it could be seen that this was a significant event that, coupled repeatedly with similarly significant events, would produce change.

Another illustration of early decisions is seen in the following case example.

Case Example

Karen, a 43-year-old professional woman, married for 25 years and with two grown children, could not tolerate anything out of place or anything unclean about herself. In her family relationships Karen was the "neat freak," and her need for order and cleanliness interfered with any fun or pleasure the family could have together. In therapy she related an incident about how she noticed a spot on her blouse and "had to" go out and buy a new blouse in order to get through the rest of the workday. Ruth, the therapist, hearing this story and noticing Karen's extreme discomfort and self-diminishing words, was able to help her connect to the unbearable shame of having acne vulgaris at age 13 and then the shame she continued to experience about her still deeply scarred face. Moreover, this feeling recycled incidents in her early childhood in which she was continuously ridiculed by other kids because of her crossed eyes. Karen's early decision was that she was ugly and couldn't be loved because of how she looked. When blemished in any way, even with a spot on her blouse, she would get anxious and need to act instantly to "get rid of" this mark of shame.

In focusing on early decisions in relationship therapy, we consider the potential impact of the early decision on the interpersonal process of the couple or family. We carefully locate those central behaviors and beliefs that are revealed in the present and that signal archaic decisions representative of the person's model of herself or himself and the outside world. We notice the imprint of an early decision in a person's posture, demeanor, voice tone, choice of words, and repetitive behaviors. We then guide patients toward recognizing the significance of the early decisions and making redecisions that will have the greatest positive effects on the relationship problem and the current dysfunctionality.

Some relationship problems do not require that individuals actually do the work of Stage II. Also, of course, some relationships do not tolerate the emotions intrinsic in an individual doing the family-of-origin work of this stage. However, we have found that it is always helpful to identify, at least verbally, the early childhood decisions that determine an individual's here-and-now interactions.

Discovering the early decision and then making a redecision means that patients reveal themselves to themselves and also to another person or persons in their relationship, while at the same time experiencing the extreme difficulty and untold vulnerability of the unmasking. The redecision process (Guideline 9) requires a safe environment that is positively focused and utilizes the patient's intact strengths. The therapeutic process is one of patience, listening, education, and support while individuals discover their old feelings and cognitive view of themselves and then replace these with updated and emotionally, behaviorally, and intellectually integrated ones.

The following case vignette demonstrates the process of the redecision work done with a young woman who participated in an intensive group therapy experience for women as the individual therapy part of the couples contract for change. Therapy with the couple when they were both present in the room remained so unsafe that it was necessary to separate Marilyn from Nick in order to make it possible for her to look at herself and discover the strength she needed to make important changes.

Case Example

Marilyn, 33 years old, was the mother of an 8-month-old daughter, Susie, born after Marilyn had lost six children to miscarriage and stillbirth. Nick, Marilyn's husband, 35 years old, worked for his family business for $10 an hour. He had a cocaine habit that cost $400 to $500 per week. Marilyn reported that they were about to lose their home "because I haven't worked since Susie's birth." Their house had been raided twice by a SWAT team looking for drugs and weapons.

Marilyn experienced herself as having no choices in her situation. She loved Nick almost "like a mother would" and was oblivious to any responsibility he might have had in their current problem—"He does his best; what more should anyone expect?"

Marilyn, the oldest of three girls, had been the "parentified" child—the one who had been made into the parent—in a family in which there had been three generations of sexual abuse, alcohol, and lying. She had taken care of her sisters since she was 8 years old, when her mother made a serious suicide attempt and was hospitalized. Though she admitted having felt frightened and inadequate when she was young, Marilyn said there had been no choices for her: she had to stay there and do the best she could—an assessment understandably true when she was a child.

Marilyn first questioned herself for just staying there with Nick in the middle of danger after other women in the group said that they would leave if they were in her place. "I don't even see it that way," she said defensively, followed by, "But I wonder why?"

Ruth asked Marilyn what she remembered about a time when she was young and others saw danger but she didn't. Marilyn quickly got a stunned, glazed look on her face, her body trembled, and tears cascaded down her cheeks.

MARILYN (*quietly*): Just the other night when Susie and I were watching TV, I saw this show where there was a bad guy chasing a mother and her little girl. The mother pushed the little girl ahead of her, away from the danger. I couldn't understand it, because I always thought that a mother was supposed to get out first. (*Tearfully*) I don't know why I am so upset. You guys must really think I'm stupid. I know this is all so dumb.

RUTH: It's okay, Marilyn, we're here and we're interested in what you're saying. The TV program must have triggered something important in you. What do you remember about having to stay behind when you were a little girl and your mother getting away first?

MARILYN (*trembling*): There were lots of times. But once—I guess I was about six or so—my mom and I stopped to look at this old abandoned house. We thought maybe we could fix it up or something because the place where we were all living wasn't so great. We looked through all of the rooms and then went outside to the porch and started looking around. I was kneeling, or something, on the porch. (*Marilyn is shaking and crying, gasping for breath; a group member puts a caring hand on her shoulder.*)

RUTH: It's safe to go ahead, Marilyn. We will be here until you have finished.

MARILYN (*glancing up momentarily*): . . . and I looked up and saw my mother running away toward the car. I yelled to find out what was wrong with her, but she kept going, even right past the car. I got up and turned around and there . . . there was a man with this huge face in the window and he had a gun. (*Hesitantly, with a terrified expression*) I didn't know what to do, and so I tried to run. I was scared and I fell, and I was bleeding, but I finally got to the car and hid behind a tire. I was worried about my mom and if she was hurt. She didn't come back for a long time, and . . . (*now almost yelling through her gasps*) and I knew I had done something stupid and wrong.

RUTH: Marilyn, you didn't do anything wrong, and you are not stupid. In fact, just think for a moment. If you, the mom, and Susie, the little girl, were caught in that very place, do you think you would run away and leave your little girl standing alone in the middle of danger?

MARILYN (*startled, looks up and replies, quickly and strongly*): No! I would make sure Susie got away first. That's what mothers are supposed to do, isn't it?

RUTH: Yes, mothers are supposed to help and protect their children.

MARILYN: But I always . . . my mom, I mean she couldn't help it, and I could take care of it . . .

RUTH: Parents are supposed to help and protect their children. You were a child, and you needed help and protection.

MARILYN (*questioningly*): You mean, my mother should have—? No, it was different for her. Or yes, maybe you're right . . . um, no, no, it wasn't . . . (*Marilyn goes back and forth for several minutes, and then speaks*) They didn't leave their little girl on the TV show, and I wouldn't leave Susie. So maybe I shouldn't have been left there either. It wouldn't be Susie's fault? Could it have been . . . no, it couldn't have been my stupid fault. No, it wouldn't be Susie's fault. It wouldn't be her fault. She wouldn't be wrong. I would be stupid and wrong if I left her. (*Bursting into loud sobs*) Maybe it wasn't me that was stupid. I needed help, I was a child.

Marilyn continued to cry for a long while and was comforted by a group member. When she left group that evening, she said, "I know something very different about me from the inside now." In the confidential and safe environment of the women's group, Marilyn had been able, one step at a time, to feel safe enough to question her current circumstances. With the support and awareness of others, she began to wonder about things in her current life. Then, with the trigger provided by the television program and the group support, Marilyn recalled a scene to illustrate her early decision.

Marilyn had been a terrified child living in the midst of danger; her early decision was literally to grow up quickly and figure it all out in order to escape danger. She could trust only herself. And since she had to take care of her mother and sisters, if anything went wrong, she believed she was stupid and incompetent.

Marilyn's redecision asserted that she was actually smart and had done the best she could as a little girl. After that redecision was made, she allowed herself to see the need to move away from danger with her young daughter. The couple therapy was completed after Marilyn's redecision. The redecision Marilyn had made quickly reverberated throughout her life and helped her to change herself and the life of her child in significant ways. She began to be able to see the grim reality of her life with Nick. She stopped turning against herself—blaming and calling herself stupid. Instead, she questioned and noticed, and then sought help. Finally, believing that she and her daughter deserved to be safe and protected, Marilyn was able to leave Nick. For a time Marilyn and Susie were under police protection. They are now living safely in their own place. Nick is still abusing drugs.

Stage III: Reintegration

An individual who has made a redecision will be different within the couple or family relationship, and this will therefore create a change in the relationship dynamics. After all, life changed significantly for Cinderella and her stepfamily when she decided to stop cleaning the hearth and become a princess.

People often need help and support in adjusting to both the system and the individual changes that have been made. Even with couples and families in which, for some reason or another, the individual work is not initiated or else not completed, it is important to move into reintegration and complete the therapy with strength and a healthy focus toward the future.

In Stage III of RRT, people in relationships have the opportunity, now that the old dysfunctional interactions have been recognized and changed, to learn new ways of interacting and being with one another (Guideline 10) (Table 4–4).

With any form of therapy or any move in life, there are destinations that define the journey. In relationship therapy the patients' visions of what is "healthy" for them are used to define the overall direction of the work. In Stage III the model combines the individual relationship vision with research work on healthy relationships. In this stage the focus is on teaching the couple or family the skills they need in order to address and manage whatever life brings. Strong emphasis is given to the concept of family and individual resilience—the ability to survive in the midst of adversity and rebound from crisis. The therapist becomes an educator, a coach, and a mentor.

In this final stage we also help people learn how to have fun and how to do well together in life. We include teaching rules of operation for relationships that allow for this healthy emotional tone to continue and grow. (These rules—no secrets, surprises, lies, distractions, excuses, or illusions—were defined in Chapter 3.) We encourage the development of healthy executive functions and mastery of the tasks of life.

Stage III is about cultivating mutual positive regard within the relationship. Shared beliefs, values, and visions foster confidence so that through the teamwork of the relationship those involved can be helped to withstand the coming storms and challenges while also enjoying together the pleasures ahead.

The research-based guidelines for healthy relationships presented in Chapter 3 (see discussion of Guideline 10) are used extensively in Stage III to aid relationships in developing new ways of operating.

Eddie and Pauline exemplify persons who have achieved an admirably healthy emotional tone in a relationship in which—

TABLE 4–4. **Redecision Relationship Therapy: Stage III therapy tasks**

Build a new shared vision.

Develop new skills.

Form new patterns of interacting.

Practice and support the new ways of being and interacting.

paraphrasing the words of Sidney Jourard when defining intimacy—people know each other, care for and about each other, respond to each other, and respect each other (5). The following is part of an interview with Eddie and Pauline just before their 65th anniversary celebration.

LES: What advice would you give all of us about creating and keeping a healthy relationship?

EDDIE: Keep your temper.

PAULINE: Keep your love. Keep your love going. Do the things that you always did when you were younger. Be fun.

LES: What I hear then is, Keep your temper so you keep the negative "stuff" down. Keep your love going by keeping the positive "stuff" up. Is this correct?

EDDIE: That's right. I tell you, the—

PAULINE: Try to have fun together.

EDDIE: We've done many things during our married life that we enjoyed so much, traveled a lot, and we have memories together—some with people and incidents that bring back such good memories. And we enjoy now just thinking about what happened.

PAULINE: And you know what, thinking about sex and all that. If we are out in a movie or a show or listening to something very romantic, invariably without thinking he will reach for my hand or I'll reach for his hand . . . without thinking, even.

EDDIE: I'll tell you another thing—

PAULINE (*reaching for his hand*): I'd get annoyed if he didn't put his hand out. I'd get annoyed. Once in a great while he doesn't, and I'll tell him.

LES: Eddie, tell me the other thing.

EDDIE: The other thing is that in our later years we have gone through physical problems. Now, these could be a disaster, but we have a way of just being together and . . .

PAULINE: Accepting them . . .

EDDIE: How should I . . .

PAULINE: Accepting them . . .

EDDIE: It's more than accepting, but actually being there and doing anything to ease the problem, the physical problem. Anything for easing your problem. She is reaching 87, and I am going to be 89 in July. So it comes naturally to us to be together 65 years.

In summary, Redecision Relationship Therapy integrates an interpersonal and intrapersonal perspective. It stresses the dignity of all persons in a relationship and recognizes their ability to change. As a treatment approach, the model is action oriented, allowing the therapist to infuse vitality and humor into the process, emphasize the positive, and utilize the strengths that each relationship can bring to the therapeutic situation.

■ REFERENCES

1. Goulding M, Goulding R: Changing Lives Through Redecision Therapy, 3rd Edition. New York, Grove Press, 1997
2. Goulding R, Goulding M: Power Is in the Patient. San Francisco, CA, TA Press, 1978
3. Berne E: The Structure and Dynamics of Organizations and Groups. New York, Ballantine, 1961
4. Nathanson D: Shame and Pride. New York, WW Norton, 1992
5. Jourard S: The Transparent Self. New York, Van Nostrand Reinhold, 1971

THE PRACTICE OF REDECISION RELATIONSHIP THERAPY

In this chapter we present two actual case histories: one representing marital or couple therapy, and one representing family therapy. Here you will see the "stuff" that relationship therapy is made of—options, options, and more options. How the therapist views the interactions played out "in vivo" determines the interventions that are made. We hope that you will learn from our choices as therapists as we tell the following stories of two brief courses of treatment.

■ THE WINSLOWS: COUPLE THERAPY

The case summarized here clearly shows how it is possible to use systems interactions not only as a base for interpersonal interventions but also as a bridge to the intrapsychic world of the individual.

Joan and Tom Winslow had been married for 8 years. It was the first marriage for both. They had chosen not to have children and had no regrets about their decision. When they came to see us, Joan was 40 years old and Tom was 37. They had initially met at a ski-club outing, and until recently their marriage had been centered around having fun together. Both Tom and Joan said they wanted to stay together. Each considered the other the only person they had in life to count on. Since both came from small families, there was little or no family-of-origin contact for either of them.

Tom initiated the therapy contact after a fellow driver mentioned to him that his marriage had changed a lot after he and his wife had seen Ruth. Tom, who operated large earth-moving equipment, had been complaining about "feeling deserted" since Joan had started law school almost a year before. Primarily, though—as Tom stated it—he always liked taking advantage of "freebies," so the four free sessions paid for by his company's employee assistance program (EAP) was what brought him to therapy.

At the first session the EAP limits for therapy were outlined. Then, after some information about the perceived problem was gathered, the contract for increasing intimacy was established, with the vehicle for reaching the goals defined as lessening the conflict and the distance between Tom and Joan. The distance and conflict would be replaced by an increasing ability to reveal themselves and talk to each other about important things. The contract framed the direction of the work, and the three-stage model offered the structure. A summary of the therapy accomplished with this couple is presented in Table 5–1.

Here is an excerpt of the actual dialogue from the second session with Tom and Joan. The focus was on getting them to talk directly with each other, outlining the difficulties appearing in the here and now, and identifying the roots of the current problem, which resided in the past histories of both Tom and Joan.

RUTH: You have both stated that the problem between you is not being able to talk to each other anymore. Tom, as an experiment, turn to Joan and tell her the most important thing she can do differently to help you and be a more supportive partner.

TOM (*turning*): To be more understanding of what I am going through at the moment and not be so judgmental and so final about everything.

JOAN: What do you mean?

TOM: I think there is a very thick wall there with you, and it is made of bullet-proof glass in the form of criticizing me. You close me out, and even when I hit you with a bullet, I can't get through to you.

RUTH: So you experience that Joan shuts you out. Do you know why she does that?

TOM: I suppose she is mad at me. But then she is always mad at me and I feel guilty, like I did something wrong . . . and I feel angry too.

RUTH: Are you angry at yourself or angry at her?

TOM: At both of us. It seems like I am always doing something wrong, like wiping the sink wrong or some other dumb thing. She knows everything that is right, and there is always something wrong with me. She shuts me out totally. She thinks I am somebody else or something.

RUTH: Joan, do you think Tom is correct about what he says about you shutting him out and always criticizing him?

TABLE 5–1.	The Winslow couple: summary of therapy
Therapy format	Four sessions (managed-care contract)
Presenting problem	Anger and distance between the partners
Therapy contract	Increased openness and intimacy
Session 1	Making contact
	Acquiring systems information and individual data relevant to the presenting problem
	Framing a contract
Session 2	Intervening in the system through structured communication
	Identifying the roots of the current problem
	Keeping the focus positive
	Completing original contract
	Formulating new contract, and family taking action
Sessions 3 and 4	Continuing communication and support
	Organizing and setting up community resources
	Termination

JOAN: Yes, I think he is, actually.

RUTH: Would you like to talk now about what goes on for you when you do this?

JOAN: No, I don't want to say.

RUTH: Tom, would you say that she was shutting you out right now?

TOM: Yes, that's right. She acts like I am a nothing or even below that.

RUTH: That sounds really strong. I wonder, Did someone else in your life also shut you out—maybe when you were young and growing up?

TOM: My mother did all of the time.

RUTH: How did she do that?

TOM: She ignored everything. And my father, of course—he just decided to disappear and be gone. So, it would be closer to ask who didn't shut me out than who did.

RUTH: Okay, then shutting you out is what you are saying you are most sensitive to. And so when Joan shuts you out, this also triggers all the old hurts—like being abandoned by your dad, and your mother ignoring you. Does that make any sense to you?

TOM (*looking down and with a cracking tone*): Uh huh, and including my grandfather dying. I needed him the most, because he was the only man in my life that meant anything good to me.

RUTH: Okay. This is the kind of thing that your wife needs to know about you: "What is really the most hurtful for me is when you shut me out, because it brings up all this old stuff."

TOM: I never thought about what it brings up until you actually pointed it out and asked who shut me out. I never thought about who shut me out before this.

RUTH: It is sometimes a very useful way to look at it—that something which is really troublesome to you in the present triggers the hurt from the past. So then you are having to handle multiple situations and feelings, and then it is easy to see your wife as if she were a critical and uncaring mother or an abandoning father.

TOM (*thoughtfully*): That's a good point.

RUTH (*turning now to Joan*): Joan, what do you think when you hear this from Tom?

JOAN (*rather defiantly*): I think I've probably been hurting him for a long time. I think I know shutting him out is hurtful and I use it as a button.

RUTH: You use it as a button. What do you mean?

JOAN: Well, if there is something that I don't want to talk about, I just don't. And I think I use it to get back at him when I am mad at him, because I know it really hurts and ticks him off. I'm mad at him for a lot of things, and nothing that I say seems to matter.

RUTH: You know, of course, that it's okay to be mad at the one you care most about, but it's not okay to get back and intentionally do things to hurt your partner?

JOAN: Yeah. I think we need to try to get to that supportive-partner deal. We haven't been there for a very long time.

TOM: A very long time.

RUTH: Joan, what is the most important thing that Tom can change for you? Will you tell him?

JOAN (*haltingly and looking away from Tom*): We agreed not to talk about this . . . but, Tom, I have to or we might as well not come here at all. And I just learned that if I don't, I'll get back at you in some way. I believe that I can't stay with you unless you get clean. Having you get clean is the only thing you can change for me. Nothing else is important.

TOM (*agitated and furious*): Am I supposed to respond?

RUTH: Do you want to respond?

TOM (*defensively*): No, not to her, but I'll tell you . . . Actually, it used to be a lot worse than it is. I used to escape from the memories, from physical pain, from a lot of injuries that I have had in my life. It's like an anesthetic for me . . . especially now that she is not around very often. You know, she is always studying or at a class or something. I am very uncomfortable at night. I have a lot of back and neck pain from some major injuries, and I have the nightmares that I've had all my life. The cocaine is an effective drug for taking away the pain of whatever it may be—physical, emotional, or whatever. It is convenient.

RUTH: As you know, the problem with that is that it brings on other pains. Have you ever gotten any help with this?

TOM: Sure, but I didn't get anything out of it. I didn't have much in common with the people who were there at the place where I went. And I don't use it as an excuse for not being able to succeed or take care of my family or do my job or anything else. (*Looking at Joan and angry*) I knew you would bring this up. I can never trust you. You always act so holy. I don't know why I even care about this marriage.

RUTH: Tom, would you ask Joan why this has become such a central issue for her?

TOM (*caustically*): So why?

JOAN: It really changes you. You get really short-tempered, and you don't seem to want to talk about much of anything. It worries me that you act different, and I don't feel that I can be very close to you. I don't think that you can be very close to me, either. You get terribly mean with me and sometimes do dangerous things, like leave the stove on. It would help a lot if we could at least talk about it.

TOM: Uh huh.

JOAN: You say you use very rarely. But you don't do laundry, and I do. And I find the spoons in your socks. It's pretty obvious.

TOM: Sometimes it's not for months and months, and sometimes it's all day.

RUTH: Tom, will you respond to Joan about talking about it? What your wife said would be helpful to her is that it not be hidden and that you could talk about it.

TOM (*to Joan*): The best thing is to talk about it more, but also be more respectful and more understanding and communicative on your part. You're worse than I am because you are always shutting down or blaming so much.

JOAN: How can I be more understanding?

TOM: You could just be willing to talk more.

JOAN: That's true. One of the reasons I don't like to talk about it is that you get mad when I want to talk about it and then you say everything is my fault.

TOM: That's usually because of the way that you present it. Tell me straight and kind what you want.

JOAN (*looking directly at Tom*): Well, what I want is for you to get help again for the drug problem. I don't see how we can ever be together much if this goes on, because I get farther and farther away from you and I don't like you then . . . and I never want to have sex with you or anything else.

This interactive sequence is an excellent example of how defining the therapy in a positive framework of being more supportive partners can help couples begin to talk about the real and underlying issues in their relationship. It shows how the core beliefs and experiences of the past reappear in the present and become barriers to intimacy. By defining the roots of the current relationship problem, the therapist is then able, through providing education and support, to help individuals take caring responsibility for themselves and the issues they bring to the current relationship struggles.

The remaining two sessions with Tom and Joan were spent on the mechanics of helping Tom get into a residential treatment program. Since he was a driver of large equipment, it was necessary to inform his employer of the substance abuse problem. To say the least, Tom was not pleased about having to do this. However, he went along with it voluntarily because he wanted to keep both his relationship with Joan and his job.

Tom's company was supportive of a residential treatment program, and Joan participated in its family component. Tom continues now in a community support program. Joan is studying for the bar exam.

Every relationship therapy case is different. And every situation challenges the relationship therapist in a different way. The Winslows were bound by the dictates of the EAP, so the challenge was to help them quickly and efficiently reach a healthy resolution to their difficulties. The next case example, involving the Matthews family, presents totally different dynamics and relationship problems—and therefore a different set of challenges and rewards.

■ THE MATTHEWS FAMILY: FAMILY THERAPY

Initial Contact: Phone Conversations

Jeannie, a well-known and highly respected local professional, called us in early May to say that she was deeply concerned about her grandnephew Paul. His school performance in the eighth grade was so bad that he was flunking almost all of his classes, and there was a serious question whether he would be able to graduate from middle school in June. Once quite close to Paul when he was younger, Jeannie found she couldn't talk with him anymore. She wanted to refer him and his family—he was currently living with his father (Jeannie's sister's son) and stepmother—for therapy with us. She had called us directly to find out if we were willing and able to see these family members. Anticipating that it would be a hard sell to get them to come in at all, she wanted to make sure of our availability. At the end of this call we asked Jeannie to have Paul's father—Jeannie's nephew Roger—call us directly.

Three days later, Roger phoned. At this time we learned that the Matthews family consisted of Roger (age 37), Melinda (36), Paul (14), Frank (5), and Cindy (3). Roger said that he had lived with his Aunt Jeannie from the age of 13 to age 24. Paul, Roger's son from his first marriage, had even lived with both Aunt Jeannie and his parents when he was very young. Melinda, Paul's stepmother, had cared for Paul since he came to live with them at the age of 9. Frank and Cindy were the biological children of Roger and Melinda. The information from the genogram was collected in a later session. However it may be useful to present it now in order to clarify the nature of the relationships (see Figure 5–1).

The family's big problem, as described by Roger over the phone, was, of course, only Paul. He was flunking his classes because of laziness and unwillingness to do his schoolwork. At home he was withdrawn and belligerent, or else he acted like a 5-year-old and punched his little brother and sister around. Roger said that he and Melinda had been good parents. They had tried everything they could to help Paul "straighten out," and now they were willing to bring him in to see us.

We decided to include Roger, Melinda, and Paul in the first session. Roger seemed eager to come in with Paul but was very reluctant to include Frank and Cindy. The kids would be scared, he said; also, it would be impossible to get anything done with them present. And, in addition, Melinda didn't want them there because "the problem really doesn't include them."

In making the initial contact, it is important to "meet" the family on their conditions. If we found it necessary to include the "little ones," or even Roger and Paul's "Aunt Jeannie," that could always happen in the future. Our first meeting was scheduled for a Saturday morning, because that was the time that best accommodated the family members. Finally, it was established that Roger and Melinda would pay 20 dollars per session. Aunt Jeannie had offered to cover the remainder of the therapy cost.

Session One

The family arrived at the office on time. Roger came from work, and Melinda and Paul came from home. As all three sat down on a rounded couch, Roger positioned himself directly in the center, extending his arms and legs into a large space around him. Paul turned out to be a tall, strapping 14-year-old. He was wearing pants

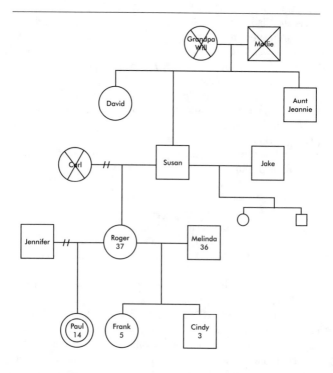

FIGURE 5–1. **The Matthews family genogram.**

five sizes too big and a reversed baseball cap. In the beginning, he never seemed to look up from his exposed navel. After introductions, the family was asked to "talk together" about why they were here and how they thought we might help them. A summary of what was accomplished in therapy in each session is provided in Table 5–2.

Roger began by loudly and angrily yelling at Paul, saying that he never talked to him or Melinda and that he was doing poorly in school because he was just so lazy. Neither Paul nor Melinda responded. Ruth decided to interrupt Roger's tirade and refocus the interaction by looking directly at Paul and asking him what he was thinking about when his father yelled.

PAUL (*smiling and looking down*): They want me to do the work, but they can't make me hand it in. And this is usual . . . he yells all of the time.

ROGER: Paul's most recent comment was, "You can beat me into doing my homework, but you can't make me like it or hand it in."

MELINDA: He often doesn't . . . but you've gotten better about that this last week, Paul.

PAUL: I'm doing my homework now and asking my teacher what I can do to bring up my grades.

ROGER (*negatively, to Paul*): Because it is the end of the year and you want to pass, though probably you won't even make that now.

RUTH (*directly to Paul*): That's real smart to try to pass.

PAUL: I want to pass because I want to be with my friends. I don't care about what he wants.

MELINDA: That's more than he has said in 3 months. What we really want is for Paul to talk to us more so we know who we are living with.

This beginning look at the family interactions provided important systemic information that we would use to guide the next

TABLE 5–2. **The Matthews family: summary of therapy**

Therapy format	Eight sessions
Presenting problem	Paul's school failure and noncommunication
Therapy contract	To help the family help Paul in different ways
Session 1	Making contact
	Helping the family be interactive
	Acquiring systems data and information about the presenting problem
	Formulating a homework assignment
Session 2	Checking homework
	Clarifying relevant DSM-IV Axis I and II information
	Gathering more data about the special circumstances of the family
	Reframing the system and individual problems
Session 3	Establishing a working contract
	Supporting and reinforcing new behaviors
	Linking current affect and dysfunctional behavior to early experiences, including abuse
	Using past data to strengthen and support current relationships
	Defining therapy gaps
Session 4	Carrying out individual assessment
	Gathering additional individual and systems data
	Focusing on younger children
	Setting the stage for future interactions
Session 5	Reinforcing new behaviors, and family following through
	Paul's making individual redecision
	Supporting different affective interactions
Session 6	Reinforcing new ways of connecting and interacting
	Supportively dealing with current losses

(continued)

TABLE 5–2.	**The Matthews family: summary of therapy** *(continued)*
Session 7	Supporting new behaviors as individuals change beliefs about themselves
	Supporting decisions about the future that are congruent with how individuals are changing
Session 8	Providing support and reinforcement
	Termination

interventions. We saw the patterns of how they responded and didn't respond to one another, in the way no one dealt directly with Roger. We also heard the family's main want for being in therapy: for Paul to change.

By the middle of this session, Paul was making eye contact with Ruth and Les and seemed to perk up every time either of them listened to him or said something positive to or about him. This, of course, was in total contrast to his father's negativism and Melinda's noncontact and careful middle-of-the-road course.

As this session neared the end, we directed ourselves to redefining the presenting problem in a way that each member of the family could accept and thereby take responsibility for some part of the change. We were also interested in creating a relevant "homework" assignment to be accomplished outside of the therapy session and before the beginning of the second session. Here is what was done.

LES: Roger, I noticed how angry you were with Paul and how much you would like him to do things differently. Will you turn to Paul now and say this to him?—"The thing that I find hardest is that you don't let me help you by being a friend, a father, or a mentor."

ROGER (*facing Paul, and with a softer tone*): You don't let me help you or let me be a father . . . But it's not only me, it's everyone. It is just that you don't seem to want to let anybody in, and that's the hardest thing for me.

RUTH: Paul, will you respond to what your dad just said?

PAUL (*hiding a tear*): What am I going to respond?

RUTH: Whatever is right for you.

PAUL (*looking down at his navel*): I guess . . . maybe you might be right, but I don't get it about why.

ROGER (*looking at his son*): I like to hear that.

LES (*to Roger and Melinda*): Think about things in this new way over the next weeks: Paul doesn't have a way of letting you in and letting you be close. He has built up all these barriers and walls and is scared to say what is real for him. So when Paul is talking and telling you about what he thinks, be sure to listen and hear what he actually says to you. See if you can get to more of his thinking about things. I think he is very bright and that he has a lot he wants to tell you. And, after all, knowing Paul is one of the goals you had by coming here.

ROGER (*with Melinda nodding assent*): That sounds right.

RUTH (*turning directly to Paul*): I'm interested in what you think about school and your own learning. Here's a short, 9-minute videotape about some possibilities of other school choices and learning programs. Next week we will start by talking about what you want with regard to your school program. You are obviously a very thoughtful young man, and I am interested in you and what it is that you want. (*Turning to Roger and Melinda*) Hold back and wait to see what Paul comes up with on his own.

PAUL (*looking straight at his parents*): Okay, I'll do it.

The Matthews' presenting problem—the problem with Paul—was redefined in positive terms. All three system participants were assigned new roles and given responsibility for following through with some part in the assignment.

Session Two

The session began by the therapists' checking to see how the assignment had worked. Paul, of course, had not watched the video, and Roger had been yelling at him about it for the last 3 days. Paul was full of blustering excuses, Roger was angry and hostile in his posture and tone, and Melinda was attempting to calm them both. Nothing was different.

Les began by addressing Paul directly and gently searching for information regarding his avoidance of school work and learning. From asking a few pointed questions, it quickly become clear that Paul's school problems were intentional and defiant and not based in learning difficulties. He was angry at his father for not accepting him and for always trying to control his life and not letting him do what he wanted. Paul's anger was manifested in his behavior—by not doing what his father most wanted from him. This, of course, was in spite of the cost to Paul himself.

Shortly after this clarification, Ruth redirected the conversation by asking Paul, Roger, and Melinda for information about Paul's mother. In the initial session it had become clear that she played an integral part in Paul's thinking and life, and we were missing essential information in this important area.

> ROGER (*responding defensively*): The last two-thirds of Paul's life has been extremely consistent with me. The only downside was when we lost our house in the earthquake and we had to rebuild and move for a while. The only source for Paul's problem now is his mother, and she has always been unreliable and a druggie.
>
> RUTH: It must be difficult for you and your son and Melinda, then.
>
> MELINDA: We have had a real hard time getting together with Paul's mom and working things out in an amicable, reasonable, truthful way. She is always trying to lure Paul away from here to take care of her. She promises

him all sorts of things and then never does anything.

RUTH: Paul, it sounds like there is a struggle. How do you see things?

PAUL: I was thinking about how my mom was trying to get me to live with her and stuff.

RUTH: Uh huh.

PAUL: But I realize something right now that I never really started realizing before: In about fifth or sixth grade, when kids started to pick on me, I just started running from them. And so I just got in the habit of running back and forth from my dad's place to my mom's place. Maybe I was just running from all of the problems with everybody, including my parents . . . all of them pulling on me and picking at me.

ROGER: You see, I think that in Paul's best interest he should live with us most of the year, and then with his mom for a little while in the summer and the holiday thing. I think that's what is actually best for him.

PAUL: Dad, I don't know if it will be best here or there, and I'm not going to do just what you want.

According to all three Matthews, Paul's mother, Jennifer, was a drug addict and her current husband was a drug dealer. Paul had five older step-siblings. Two of them were currently in prison; a third played in a rock band and would give Paul a job anytime he wanted; a fourth worked at a local fast-food place; and the whereabouts of the fifth was unknown.

Paul expressed a desire to be with his mother more, because sometimes she "needs my help . . . plus, they don't ever criticize me there." Since he was 14, Paul could actually choose where to be. But he said he really wasn't sure, "especially now that Aunt Jeannie is sick again."

Paul was torn between two loyalties, and his biological mother and father were at war, with Paul in the middle, the spoils of the battle. His school problems were partially a result of this conflict—his inability to pick sides and define his loyalty to one or the other of his parents. Roger attempted to win the war by having power over Paul, and Paul's mother offered seductive prizes of excitement, no school, and taking care of her.

We returned now to investigate another important element and relationship in Paul's young life.

RUTH: Paul, can you tell us what's important about Aunt Jeannie being sick again?

PAUL: Well, she has been just like another parent to me, but she is different because she always likes me, I can just feel it. I lived with her when I was a baby. Did you know that? My dad lived with her since he was my age, and then my mom and me and my dad, and then just me and my mom lived with her for a while.

RUTH: No, we didn't know that. It sounds like she has been a very important and safe person in your life. But what do you mean—that she is sick again?

PAUL: She always took care of us, and now (*looking down and hiding his face, with a halting voice*) she has cancer again. But I know she is going to be all right.

MELINDA: I can't believe that this is the same Paul! He never talks about this at home. It is hard on all of us. (*Her hand has stretched out to Roger and is resting on his shoulder. Roger, like Paul, is looking straight down. Paul sits alone, having pulled away.*)

This second session was brought to a close shortly after this interchange. Before concluding, we suggested to Paul that, if he chose, he might be interested in writing a note to Aunt Jeannie and telling her how important she was to him—a homework suggestion.

Both Paul and Roger obviously had a difficult time managing and expressing their feelings; Melinda was able several times to bridge the gap with her soft and caring affect. By continuing to gather relevant data about both the structure of the family and the present situation, we learned more about the multiple elements impacting the Matthews family. We were also able to continue to observe their interactions.

Our analysis at this time was this:

Roger was constantly angry and had a difficult time with any positive connections. There was an intensity behind his "going after" Paul that did not seem to fit entirely with the present circumstances.

Melinda had revealed that she too was concerned about how angry she could get. She remarked that neither she nor Roger knew much about having "all these kids" and that many times it seemed to her that she was too young to be doing all of this, especially when she "didn't even know how to drive a car." Even though Melinda had a college education, it seemed that no woman in her family had ever gotten a driver's license, and she didn't know if she ever would, despite the problems it caused Roger in having to drive her and the kids to places all the time.

At this point, the presenting problem of Paul's school problems and defiance had been successfully reframed as his inability to let people get close to him. He was confused about where he was safe and which of his two parents he really belonged with. And he was clearly very frightened about the possibility of losing his Aunt Jeannie—the one person who had helped him consistently to feel safe and good about himself. The family members accepted these interpretations, and the working contract of helping them learn new ways of helping Paul was agreed on.

Session Three

Paul began by proudly showing a copy of the letter that he had written to Aunt Jeannie and shared with us what he had said to her: how she had always been nice to him, shown him interesting things, given him money when he needed it, and helped his dad out of jams. In reading the letter, he left no question but that he was quite capable of expressing himself when given the freedom and support to do it in his own way.

Roger continued to be negative about Paul even when he heard the letter. It seemed even more clear to us that something interfered with Roger's ability to respond to his son in a caring and appropriate way. Roger's inability to change his present perspective and interaction with Paul was most certainly grounded in the past. We looked for the opportunity to link Roger's current behavior with his past, and here we got a peek at who Roger was and what his family history had been.

LES: Roger, I am wondering about your anger with Paul. You seem, on the one hand, to be very caring and to want to have a connection with him, and yet you also get so harsh and critical with him. Do you notice this about yourself?

ROGER: Yeah. A couple of times I really had to shut myself down because I would have hurt him. There's no doubt in my mind about this. I have an incredible amount of rage and am extremely strong for my size, so I could definitely do some damage.

LES: I'm really glad to hear that you know this about yourself, and I definitely think that it's best that you stop—maybe not shut down, but certainly STOP. Roger, did you get hurt as a kid?

ROGER: Uh huh. The physical stuff was a piece of cake. But it was more the mental abuse from my stepfather.

RUTH: Will you tell us what it was like?

ROGER: Yeah. I got hit with items like tools and things. And then at the dinner table, for example, when I didn't want to eat something and was forced to eat it, if I threw up, I was made to eat the vomit. There was even a special can for me. Then there were other regular things, like when I would eat what I wanted on the plate first and leave things I didn't want until last, hoping I wouldn't have to eat them. But there was a time limit on how long I had to eat. Also, if I didn't take the bites in succession, or if I took two bites of the same item or out of sequence, I would get hit in the back of the hand with a knife. And after all that, I just started wolfing down my food so I wouldn't have to deal with any of it. But then I would have to chew each bite 32 times whether there was anything in my mouth or not, and if I didn't chew it 32 times or if I lost count, I would get hit. And so that was like just one little section, just one little thing in my life that was all controlled. You know, showers were timed, and if I went over my time, I got hit and smacked around in the shower. Every little thing that I did from the time I got up to the time that I went to bed was controlled.

RUTH: I'm sorry. It must have been very difficult. How did you survive?

ROGER: I cried a lot and every night. My stepfather didn't allow my mother to say prayers with me or anything. She was only allowed to go to the other two kids, which were his. So there was that alienation as well. It was a very military kind of upbringing, you know. If I was doing something like washing the dishes or something else and he told me to empty the trash and I said, "Okay, as soon as I get done here," then he would beat me because I wouldn't do what he said fast enough or something like that. He'd send me to find a tool, and I would be so scared that I couldn't find the tool, even if it was right in front of me. And he would come get it and hit me with it. Things like that.

RUTH: Lots of years like that? Again, how did you survive all of that?

ROGER: I finally fought back. We had a war, and he let me leave. I think that if I had stayed any longer, I would

have been another childhood statistic or he would have
been a statistic. I really don't like talking about it.

RUTH: I understand that. Those are hard things to remember
and talk about.

ROGER: I just remember it all the time, all kinds of strange
things. I still throw away the last bite of my food. It
doesn't matter if I am still hungry or whatever—I just
do it. And do other things like that. When I left home,
I made up my mind that nobody was ever going to
control my life in any way again.

RUTH: I hear some things which I think are crucial. I hear
first of all that you made a decision to survive and live
and that is extremely important. In order to keep the
survival decision, you also decided never to be controlled by anyone. Does that seem right to you?

ROGER: Yeah.

RUTH: Now let's see if we can connect some things. I hear
two parts of you. I hear, first, a part of you that gets
very frustrated with Paul's not allowing you to control
his school work or his conversation with you. Second,
I hear that there is also a part of you that respects Paul's
ability to resist and survive in his own way. This is what
you did, after all. Do you realize that Paul has made the
same decision you did—he will never let you control
him?

ROGER: Wow, you are right! That reminds me of something
Melinda pointed out to me when Frank was just taking
a bite of a vegetable at the table and I started yelling at
him about how he was eating. (*He is crying openly
now*)

ROGER (*after some time*): No, they shouldn't have to deal
with anything like that. I shouldn't be like that, and
I know it.

RUTH: Yes, you are right. Neither Paul nor Frank should
have to deal with anything like that, and you shouldn't

have had to either. Abuse is wrong. You are different from your stepfather in many ways. He was abusive, and you are very insightful about yourself. I have the utmost respect and am touched by your experience and who you are. It takes a lot to admit these things about your past and to care for yourself and other people in a different way.

ROGER: Thanks.

LES: Roger, I too am touched with what I have heard and especially with your willingness and ability to look at yourself and to figure out new ways of being with yourself, your wife, and your children. Now, Paul, will you tell your dad what you think and feel as you hear those things about him? Would you look at him and tell him?

PAUL: Huh, I wasn't thinking much. I was listening to you. I was picturing what that would be like. Not good stuff, Dad. (*Roger is just sitting with his head down and makes a slight nod to acknowledge Paul's connection to him.*)

LES: Not good stuff.

PAUL: No. And the real sick stuff is that if I asked that old guy about it, he wouldn't even admit that he ever did it to my dad.

LES: What goes on inside of you when you hear all of this?

PAUL: That I am glad that my life isn't like that, and that I want to beat that old ——— to the ground myself.

In this session we learned more about Roger and his past. He was able to talk about the abuse and had spoken for the first time to his wife and son about what his childhood had been like. He recognized his early decision to keep himself tightly in control in order to survive and to get out as soon as possible. He would never let himself be controlled again. Roger also had made insightful connections between his past and his present way of being. He was strongly affected by the awareness of his own critical and abusive tendencies and how easy it would be for him to become like his stepfather. He recognized how he could repeat his past with his own kids, even though he was determined not to.

Roger's recognition of his early decision and how it had served him in the past, combined with his ability to see how he was currently repeating old behaviors, led him to a redecision about being different in the present. Roger redecided that attempting to have power over Paul was wrong and he didn't want to repeat his stepfather's actions. He would now let Melinda and us help him learn ways to have personal power that were not harmful to himself or others.

Our concern at the close of this session was whether Roger would feel shame for having revealed so much about his past and his inner self. People often need a period of withdrawal in order to recover and rebuild after allowing themselves to be so vulnerable.

The importance of Aunt Jeannie to the family unit also emerged again in this session. Her illness and apparently impending death were certain to have an immense effect on this family; she had provided the safe haven and nurturing for both Roger and Paul in their early years. (Aunt Jeannie had cared for Roger until her sister had married his stepfather when Roger was 5 years old.) And when Roger left home as a teenager to be with Jeannie, he was only 7 months younger than Paul was now. He lived with Aunt Jeannie from that point forward, until his first marriage broke up. Through the years she had continued to care for and about them both.

At this point in the therapy all of the necessary data had been acquired except for the missing piece of Melinda. Recognizing this gap defined the initial focus for the next session. It should be mentioned that Paul continued to plunge ahead with trying to rescue himself at school and to graduate with his friends.

Session Four

Today only Melinda was present. Paul (as we had previously known) was off for a long weekend with his mother. Roger was working swing shift and had just returned home. "He could have come but didn't really want to," Melinda said. This was what we had been concerned about. Therefore, Les immediately took time away from the session to call Roger, with the intent to make contact, establish the time of the next session, and bridge the relationship gap.

This session would be profitably used now alone with Melinda, to explore her past, her feelings about herself, and her view of how things were going with Paul. It was also time to gather information about the younger children. Melinda proved a willing participant and in fact even seemed relieved to be alone. This in itself was important systems information, since questions such as "Why does Melinda hold back so often when Roger is present?" were still unanswered directly.

Melinda began by saying, "Raising three kids is a difficult job for me. Roger was absolutely correct when he said that we are like little-kid parents." Melinda went on to say that she had concerns—especially about Frank, who was having difficulties in school and also in getting along with his friends. He was never able to sit still and bounced all over the place. He was also sometimes "too much of a baby." In exploring this, Melinda expressed particular fear that because her grandmother on her mother's side had a manic-depressive illness, Frank "could have gotten it." Moreover, she was also concerned about herself: she often got very angry and yelled wildly, as she remembered her grandmother doing.

Melinda was asked to talk with people at the school about Frank, and we coached her on things to look for and questions to ask regarding him. We gave her a simple evaluation questionnaire and instructed her to get five people, including Frank's teacher and her and Roger, to answer it. We would put the information together as soon as we received it.

It turned out that Melinda's grandmother had lived with her when she was growing up. It had been very frightening for her, so she could well understand how Frank and Cindy and Paul would be frightened when she and Roger were yelling—which they did a lot, she said. Melinda saw herself as easily getting out of control and not having the ability to manage herself.

As the interview progressed, both Les and Melinda decided that medication for her was not indicated (a question that Melinda herself had raised). Les pointed out that there were many other ways for her to soothe and calm herself and thereby to take more control of her own actions and temper. These were suggested also as ways that she could help Frank calm down.

According to Melinda, Paul was doing better in school—being more responsible. He was also participating more in the family and playing better with the little kids. It was pretty clear that he would go on to the ninth grade, even though he might not qualify to take part in the graduation event itself, and therefore might not be allowed to attend the graduation ceremony dance. Since Paul very much wanted to do these things, he was currently working to meet the school requirements and join his friends. He especially wanted to be part of the limousine ride to the dance and the party after graduation.

Before this fourth session drew to a close, Melinda was asked about how different she was when Roger was not present. We commented that she seemed so much more involved and forthcoming this week when she was alone. Melinda tearfully talked about her fear and concern about Roger; he worked very hard, and his job was not going well. He was "on the edge"—she had seen it often with her grandmother and so was scared. Also, concern about Aunt Jeannie's health was devastating him, and she did not want to burden him.

A very important piece of the systems puzzle had now been uncovered. We encouraged Melinda to bring her fears and concern up with Roger at the next session, when she would get help in talking with him about herself and her fear for him. Even though frightened, Melinda saw clearly that part of being a responsible parent and a participating partner with Roger was to talk about her concerns. Melinda also made the connection that she was no longer a scared little girl living with her grandmother and that she had the power to stand up and take care of what concerned her. She concluded with a new sense of herself and a question: "Since I really am a grown-up, I need to act that way. I wonder if I could even learn to drive. That would really be taking more responsibility and helping Roger a lot."

Session Five

Melinda, Paul, and Roger were all present. Melinda was understandably proud of herself. She reported success in following through with the ways we had suggested for quieting herself and Frank. An appointment had been scheduled to consult with Frank's kindergarten teacher and the school psychologist. Roger, quieter than before, wondered what magic had happened: Melinda was beginning driving lessons, and her mother was going to get her a car. Also, the harsh edge with Paul was gone. Paul was active and initiated conversation. For the first time he was dressed differently—a new hat, pants, and shirt that he hoped to wear to graduation, if he got to go.

RUTH: Paul, how did the visit with your mother go?

PAUL (*anxious to talk, jumping right in*): I didn't exactly grow up normal, either with her or him. Only Aunt Jeannie made it like other kids for me.

RUTH: What do you mean?

PAUL: What my dad said last time, and then being at my mother's made me remember that when I was 4 years old—well, from the time I was born until I was around 5—both my parents were doing drugs. I had seen them doing drugs, both of them. I'm telling you this (*looking at his dad now*) because he told you about his father, and he said it's okay to talk about it because he stopped a long time ago. But she never stopped, not even til this day.

RUTH: Uh huh.

PAUL (*head down and with a shaky voice*): When I was four, I was taking a bath and my dad got home from a pool tournament, and when he came in he started throwing my mom around the living room. I was always protective of my mom and would bite my dad on the butt whenever he tried to hurt her like that—just like a little guard dog. And so I ran up . . . I ran up and bit him on the butt that time. He turned around and pushed me down and kicked her around really good. I ran outside and started yelling, and then the cops came and took him away. To see my dad handcuffed and taken out of the house, put in a cop car, and taken away . . . well , it isn't exactly normal. None of that is normal, is it? It always bothers me what I did, too.

RUTH: No, none of that is normal. What do you think that has to do with any of the problems that are going on now?

PAUL: Okay, that doesn't have anything to do really with schoolwork except maybe that I'm still angry at my dad, like he is with his stepfather. But I'm extremely protective of my friends and stuff now. (*Now very tense and loud*) I could probably kill someone! And if somebody ever tried to hit one of my friends or my little brother and sister, I would probably hurt them very badly—even including Melinda or my dad.

RUTH: Okay, so what you are saying, then, is how angry you are feeling inside and how scared you are of yourself and your anger.

PAUL: Basically, I don't want to be like my grandfather, but my dad didn't either and then sometimes he is.

RUTH: That's really important to know about yourself. That you are scared of your anger and that you have to stop yourself so that you don't hurt yourself or anybody else. But do you have a voice inside that says, "STOP, DON'T DO THIS!"?

PAUL: Yeah, I do, and I think I probably got that anger when

I saw my dad beating on my mom and even me because he was always criticizing me. Do you think that?

RUTH: Yes, it makes sense that you probably got that anger when you saw your dad beating on your mom. And also, I am glad to hear that you do have a very healthy voice inside that says, STOP!

PAUL: You made me think right now that I am never going to do that stuff that they did, my dad and grandfather, I mean . . . because I can say STOP and not hurt anyone.

RUTH: Paul, you are a very special and bright young man. I respect your courage and willingness to see yourself. Perhaps it will even be easier to go ahead with things you want for yourself now that you are secure with the voice that says STOP when you need it. (*Paul, Melinda, and Roger now all have tears, and Roger has reached out to his son.*)

LES: Do you think that your dad has a voice about stopping?

PAUL (*looking up and then toward his father*): He must, because he wants to beat on me a lot, I can tell that. (*And then adding quickly*) He said I could talk about this. I think he does it because he was beaten by his stepdad. I know my dad, but he never knew his dad. (*Smiling broadly*) It's different now.

LES: Roger, what are you thinking and feeling now that you have heard your son?

ROGER (*his voice cracking and with a somber expression*): When I hear Paul and look at the kids, I know I have to be able to say STOP to myself more and not be so hard on all of them. By the way, Melinda and I talked the other night, and she told me to stop also. That will help as long as I listen to her and to myself.

The session ended with the family having a very different kind of contact and interaction. Ruth and Les stayed in the background except to schedule the next appointment.

Session Six

It was a sad morning; the feeling in the room was overwhelming. Aunt Jeannie was in the hospital and not doing well. Roger hesitantly commented: "I don't know what I will ever be able to do without her. She has been the only real parent to me, because she was the only person who ever protected me. Her sister sure didn't." Roger had not been sleeping much and had been spending all his time away from the job at the hospital with her. He looked drawn and was experiencing pain in his stomach.

Paul expressed surprise that Aunt Jeannie was having to stay so long in the hospital. He was obviously having a hard time accepting the reality of her illness. "What's there to feel bad about?" Paul wondered. "Aunt Jeannie is going home soon, and everything will be fine again."

The only lightness in the session came with the joking back and forth about Melinda's having a college degree and only just now learning to drive. Paul, delighting in this, was sure he would get his license before she did.

Although Paul had "saved" some of his school credits, he was unable to attend the celebrations at the end of the school year. Paul and Roger (at our suggestion) went to a movie on the night of the graduation dance. They even sat in the car together and watched as all of Paul's friends came out of the limousine and went into the dance. "I would have been there with them if I hadn't goofed off so long," Paul acknowledged. "I will do it differently for myself next time. I'm not stupid, you know."

The family interaction had changed. The affect was more caring, and the interactions were supportive. Each person had taken a peek at themselves and, through a new understanding of who they were, had developed a different way of managing themselves—and therefore a different way of being with one another. These changes would help them work through the impending death of Aunt Jeannie in a very different way.

Session Seven

This session had been postponed for several weeks because of Aunt Jeannie's death. The Matthews had been in contact by phone, and at the request of both Paul and Roger we even visited the hospital ourselves. At the funeral, Roger was upset and unable to speak. His difficulty seemed to be a combination of feeling the loss and having to deal with the presence of his mother and stepfather.

Roger began this session, 2 weeks after the funeral, by talking further about how Aunt Jeannie had saved his life. "She gave me a place to be, to find myself, and to grow up safely," he said haltingly and with tears. Roger was relieved that he had taken the time in the last weeks to be with Jeannie and to say all of the things he wanted to say before she had gone. He had shared his love and appreciation, and Jeannie had known he was there. Aunt Jeannie's death had also evoked feelings about the death of his father, and Roger looked ahead to being more present for his children.

Paul was proud of himself for having gotten up at the funeral and spoken for both himself and his father, who was so choked up he couldn't talk. Paul, the youngest to speak, was very clear and strong in the sense that now he felt he could handle anything he wanted to.

This session focused on the Matthews' grief and the grieving process. As part of this, we told them what they might expect when someone important dies. We continued to make the bridge with Paul between his ability to control himself and his success. He was capable and had many options in his life—the choices would be his. This was a particularly important discussion because Paul was leaving the next day to go to his mother's for several weeks.

One choice of Paul's would be whether or not to go to a special learning-skills camp for the last week of the summer. He had finally watched the videotape we had lent him and was intrigued with the place. Aunt Jeannie had left an envelope with the tuition for the camp, if he decided to go.

During this session Paul decided to return in time to go to camp and then to live with Roger and Melinda. He was going to use the

STOP voice that he had learned was in his head. He seemed sure now that he could do it. His friends had been very impressed when he spoke at the funeral. The word spread quickly, and Paul got lots of positive attention. He was even considering getting on the debating team in high school. After all, he said, the team got to travel to other schools just to out-think and out-argue the competition.

Melinda's driver's test, we learned, was scheduled for the beginning of the next week.

Session Eight

This was the last scheduled session. Only Melinda and Roger were present. Three weeks had passed. Melinda was now driving on her own and very proud of herself. The family relationships were different. Roger's life was easier now because there were two drivers in the family. He had even joined a men's support group.

The younger kids benefited too from their mother's new independence. Not so confined at home, they had begun some outside activities that allowed them to meet more kids and do things away from their mother. Melinda too was beginning to make some friends outside of her mother and sister. Also, the school had assigned Frank (for the fall) to a special program for evaluating children with possible learning problems. Melinda and Roger were satisfied that they had taken appropriate action to help Frank. They had also signed up for a series of parenting classes offered in the community college's adult education series.

For a while Roger and Melinda had been concerned that Paul would not follow through on his decision to return to his father's home. As it turned out, their concern was not warranted. In the last few days, Paul had reaffirmed his plan to go to camp, and he had been making many plans with his friends for the school year beginning in the fall. He had decided to become a wrestler and to see if he could make both the wrestling and the debate teams in high school. Of course, said Roger and Melinda, they knew of these plans only because they had talked with Paul's friends. There was laughter in the session today as the adults marveled at the world of teenagers.

The focus in this, the last session, was on saying goodbye and helping Roger and Melinda work together as parents of three very different kids. Keeping their relationship working in a healthy way and getting together on their values and skills as joint parents were now of the utmost importance to them. They had learned from Jeannie's example, and then from losing her, that parenting was the most important job in their life and that they needed to get on with it.

Roger reported that he was much more secure in himself. Talking about the abuse he suffered as a child had lessened the shame that he felt about himself—and even some of the rage he felt about his stepfather. He identified his Aunt Jeannie as "the stock that I came from" and was gaining in determination to do parenting in her way, rather than the way that it had been done to him. He now talked about himself as able to learn to do it differently. As they left, Roger's eyes were damp, and he thanked us both for our help in mending his family.

PART III

SPECIAL CONSIDERATIONS IN MARITAL AND FAMILY THERAPY

6

SPECIAL POPULATIONS

In today's world the relationship therapist is faced with numerous special situations that require additional expertise. In this chapter we address only a few of the possible situations we could consider. Those we include here were chosen because either they represent the cutting edge, as in the case of using relationship approaches in the treatment of persons with chronic illness and in working with couples in gay and lesbian relationships and, in some cases, their families, or they are particularly difficult problems fraught with countertransferential meaning, as in the case of work with families with elderly members or couples with sexual difficulties. We also examine special approaches to working with children and adolescents, because, in spite of family therapists priding themselves on working with entire families, research suggests that children, even when present, are not "included." Work with the remarried family is considered because of its obvious prevalence in today's world. Substance abuse is addressed for similar reasons.

In this chapter we switch from references to selected readings. We do this because each of the subjects represents an entire specialty and we want to present an overview of the field.

■ MARITAL AND SEX THERAPY

Although marital therapy is rightly included as a subset of family therapy, the dyadic bond has enough unique features to merit special attention. Forming a partnership with another person is one of life's most important transitions. It is a marker of entrance into adulthood, yet it brings to mind the parental models of both partners.

Treating couples who are unhappy with the way they function sexually is a special branch of marital therapy. It has its own literature, language, and lexicon of interventions. We include it in this concise guide because sex should always be talked about in marital therapy, when a partner is included as part of individual therapy, or when the couple is seen as part of family therapy. The sexual relationship is, more often than not, a metaphor for the entire relationship, and relationship therapy depends on the ability to work from the perspective of the patients' metaphors.

Issues for Marital and Sex Therapy

Committed partnering presents the special challenge of walking the fine line between autonomy and dependence, a process that can be thought of as the adult-stage variation of the earlier separation-individuation developmental landmark. This issue of independence versus dependence is addressed in every form of marital theory and therapy. Bowen-derived theory addresses this conflict through its focus on "differentiating from the undifferentiated ego mass." Structural therapy addresses it in the context of boundaries between subsystems. The experiential therapies, as well as the insight-oriented therapies, address the conflict through the various forms of projection and transference. Even the psychoeducational therapies strive to facilitate independence as they teach couples how to manage their children and, in the process, how to be separate from their children and from each other.

There are, as mentioned earlier (see Chapter 3), several ways of managing the tension related to the separation-individuation conflict. Distancing, in the form of withdrawing by some form of pushing or pulling away, or triangulating, is the most common. When partners use these mechanisms in an agreed-on way, the relationship is stable. Problems develop, however, when their needs for distance and closeness are out of balance. If one person has a greater need for distance at any given time, pulling away is usually experienced as loss by the other partner, whose ensuing attempts to close the distance will often raise the conflict level.

Again, virtually all of the specific marital therapies are designed to address this dynamic. Negotiating reciprocal agreements with the partners, teaching skills to manage affect, implementing psychoeducational behavioral methods, tracking self-image as a way of facilitating individuation, directly addressing the discrepancy between the partners' level of attained separation-individuation— these are but a few of the many ways marital therapists help patients manage difficulties in sustaining a partnership.

Probably the most important aspect of marital therapy is the idea of *thinking family.* In the current context, thinking family not only applies to the concept of circular causality but also serves as a reminder that although we can focus on the couple as a dyad, many couples have children. Therefore, what we see in the office when we meet with the couple may be very different from what they experience at home when children or other family members are present.

Sex therapy, like marital and family therapy (MFT), has a long history, comprising various themes that affect our current thinking. Early studies focused on psychopathology and morality. After this early work, the focus shifted to the Freudian notions of psychosexual immaturity, then to the performance-limiting aspects of anxiety, and onto failures of learning. Most recently, the meaning of the symptom in the context of the couple's relationship has become the dominant theme. All of these themes appear to some extent in contemporary sex therapy.

In the 1990s the morality theme is ever-present, and heterosexual sex using the missionary position continues to be the gold standard with which all other forms of sexual activity are compared. The extent to which therapists accept this standard as normative, of course, affects the direction of their therapeutic interventions.

The so-called sexual revolution of the 1970s allowed people to talk more openly about many sexual practices. But in spite of the new openness, talking about sex still is often associated with shame. This applies to therapists as well as to patients. One way the shame scenario plays out is through the definition of what is "normal." When it becomes apparent that the therapist is uncomfortable talking about sex, or that his or her definition of normality is different from the patient's, therapy comes to a halt because the patient will not talk about what is troubling him or her. It follows that the single most important intervention in treating sexual problems is to *ask the questions*. Ask the questions, and get a detailed history!

Treatment Focus

Sexual problems can be viewed through many lenses. Sex is a behavior; it is what people do. Sexual difficulties can represent an individual behavioral problem, a medical problem, or both. Sex is also what people do with each other. Their interactions in the area of sexuality can be usefully described in the language of systems, and the problem can be framed in terms of a systems failure. In the context of a systems failure, when a couple is having problems, particularly sexual problems, the dynamics of power and inequality are often an important component of the problem. Finally, sexual difficulties are often the result of inadequate knowledge. Not surprisingly, we don't effectively teach or learn subjects when shame is attached to the subject matter.

DSM-IV classifies sexual problems into four main groups: disorders of desire, arousal, orgasm, and pain. The individual problems within each group can be the result of a medical problem, a relational problem, a knowledge problem, or, more likely, some combination of the three. For example, it is possible, even relatively easy, to treat primary anorgasmia in a woman with individual behavior therapy, group therapy, and psychoeducational programs. It is not always easy, however, for the newly orgasmic woman to transfer that behavior to the relationship, and the failure to be orgasmic *in the relationship* can undermine an otherwise successful treatment outcome. The same is true for premature ejaculation in the man. With this in mind, exploring the sexual difficulties in the relationship context means looking at the ways in which the problem impacts the couple and the ways the relationship impacts the problem. It is particularly true, in these and similar situations, that the main problem might not be the sexual difficulty per se—including the medical problem—but rather the couple's way of handling the difficulty.

Therefore, treatment of a medical problem alone does not always lead to a successful therapeutic outcome, because relational problems either predated the sexual problem, coexist with the sexual problem, or developed in the context of the sexual problem. More often than not, the relational difficulties are most intractable in couples who are poorly differentiated. In poorly differentiated couples, one partner will often transform the other partner's difficulties into his or her own personal failure, which over time becomes part of his or her core identity. The first step in successful treatment is for the therapist to help members of the couple separate themselves from the problem and draw their boundaries.

Drawing boundaries is important, but it is not enough. Unless each partner becomes secure in his or her own self, relapse is common. "Undesired" partners, for example, often have to accept their partner's lack of desire as intrinsic to the partner rather than as a reflection on themselves. They may have to acknowledge that a full sexual relationship will take a long time to achieve, or even that it will never happen. When "never happen" is the case, it is important to help both individuals in the relationship grieve the loss.

As we mentioned at several points in this book, it is hard to learn the basics of anything if one feels shame about one's self, one's capability, one's identity, or even one's gender. For many people, obtaining information is a key strategy in reducing anxiety; therefore, education is an important part of sex therapy. To some extent the therapist replaces the parent who did not provide the necessary information or permissions. Fortunately, there are many books, audio- and videotapes, educational programs, and support groups to facilitate the learning process. It is also important to remember that most of the changes that people make, particularly in sex therapy, occur outside the consultation room.

Case Example

When they entered marital therapy, Sue (age 52) and Bill (age 65) were in the midst of a crisis because Bill's business was in difficulty. Worried, Bill had withdrawn, leaving Sue feeling hurt and angry. Whenever they tried to talk, tempers flared, and both were considering divorce. Luckily, their relationship was basically good. They were skilled and considerate partners and responded quickly to couple therapy.

In the second session of marital therapy we asked about their sexual relationship. After a long silence they began to describe their difficulties. Both had been married before. Sue reported that she had always enjoyed sex and felt successful. On the other hand, Bill, with characteristic reticence, described a long history of premature ejaculation. Both indicated it was present but not problematic in the early part of their 10-year relationship. Lately, possibly predating Bill's emotional withdrawal, Bill had seemed less interested in sex. Bill said that he was worried that his age was a major contributing factor to his sexual difficulties.

After obtaining a sexual history from both of them, we were struck by the way Bill was following a family pattern of unassertiveness. It was also clear that the embarrassment he felt at talking about sex and his performance interfered with the couple's solving the problem themselves and also with the therapeutic process. Even though there was no indication of a medical problem, we referred Bill to a urologist to provide the information he obviously needed about himself. As we suspected, the evaluation confirmed that he was medically normal in all respects. His testosterone was normal; he had normal firm nocturnal erections, as measured by nocturnal recordings of penile tumescence; and there were no intervening medical problems. He was actually gratified to learn his testosterone level was that "of a young man."

Armed with this reassurance about himself, Bill was prepared to engage in a program that would allow him to assertively engage Sue sexually as well as nonsexually. They were given a series of exercises, including instructions to engage in massage, which focused on intimate behaviors; the postexercise reviews addressed their feelings about themselves and each other.

Throughout this work, and in keeping with Redecision Relationship Therapy (RRT), we were more interested in the interpersonal process than in the details of the exercises we assigned the couple. This principle was manifested in our attention to how Bill and Sue talked to each other about difficult subjects and to the interactions that helped or hindered the development of Bill's assertiveness. Bill typically withdrew whenever Sue was assertive. We coached Bill on what "staying present" meant and how to do it. When assertiveness was tracked as the dominant metaphor, the frequency of Bill's premature ejaculation diminished, in parallel with the rise in self-confidence as he was able to stay present during the exercises.

■ GAY AND LESBIAN FAMILIES

Gay and lesbian couples are arriving at marital and family therapists' offices with increasing frequency. Reasons for this increased use of marital and family therapy include increased openness about all aspects of their lives, a desire to maintain long-term relationships, and an apparently greater acceptance of psychotherapy in general than among heterosexual couples.

Working with gay and lesbian couples presents a special challenge to the heterosexual psychotherapist because it requires that we confront our own biases. Most of us live in a heterosexual world in which heterosexual values and attitudes are the norm and, therefore, all other values and practices are defined as abnormal. The imposition of this standard leads to misunderstanding and faulty treatment planning.

Issues for Same-Sex Relationships

Society's antigay bias has a powerful impact on the relationships of same-sex couples. The anticipation and actuality of prejudice, prejudgment, dislike, disgust, and/or aversion define at least some portion of every same-sex couple or family's way of living. For example, there is a continued belief in our culture that same-sex partners—particularly when the partners are male—have unstable relationships and provide poor role models, and therefore create sexual identity problems for any children they might have. The research clearly does not support these beliefs. Yet they continue to be so prominent and influential that it is much harder for persons in gay and lesbian relationships to raise their families, whether they were already parents when taking up a same-sex lifestyle or they decided later to create or adopt children.

Ethnicity biases also must be taken into account when one is working with same-sex couples in relationship therapy. Sex role behavior plays against the backdrop of culturally determined expectations. For example, when a Latino male with a background expectation of a machismo orientation is in a gay relationship, he must struggle with himself, his family of origin, his culture, and sometimes even his partner. Similar difficulties occur with people of African-American background.

Concerns about "coming out" to one's family of origin are also important and have tremendous impact on multiple generations of the family. Relationship therapists often define openness as the norm and believe that the resolution of intrapersonal conflict is achieved by differentiating from one's family of origin. There is no evidence, however, that coming out to one's family of origin has any positive impact on one's current relationship with a same-sex partner. In fact, being "out" sometimes creates major problems for the family of the gay person, and this in turn results in rejection of the gay or lesbian child, which further isolates the person from his or her family. Not encouraging "coming out," on the other hand, often presents an ethical dilemma for the relationship therapist who believes that lies and illusions interfere with healthy relationships. The dilemma is partly resolved by remembering that the choice is the patient's, not the therapist's, to make.

Health is a major concern for gay couples, with problems related to health striking at many levels. Although the death rate from AIDS is beginning to decrease here in the United States, the epidemic rages on. Whether or not an individual is infected to some degree determines his or her eligibility as a partner. Infidelity is a potentially life-threatening event. Caring for a sick partner is a frequent concern, and dealing with loss and grieving may become a common and significant part of the relationship. Thus, health issues inevitably enter the discourse with gay couples, and although they usually do not expect the heterosexual therapist to know as much about the illnesses or the issues as they do, they do expect the therapist to be sensitive to their concerns.

Treatment Focus

Treatment of gay and lesbian couples and families requires that many biases and beliefs of what is normative be set aside. Much of the research on relationships must be set aside as well, because research conducted on heterosexual couples does not transfer to nonheterosexual couples. For example, a belief that the heterosexually oriented therapist may face when meeting with a gay or lesbian couple is that gay and lesbian couples structure their relationships as heterosexual partners do. This belief fails to be supported. Simply noticing the different possible ways sex and gender manifest in an individual and in a relationship challenges that belief. Relationship therapists must consider the biologic sex, gender identity (one's self perception), gender role behavior as culturally defined, sexual behavior, sexual orientation (feelings of attraction), and sexual orientation identity (self-recognition of one's orientation). People can be defined and define themselves differently in all of these areas, and these differences often meet in one couple.

We are also beginning to recognize an additional pattern in which an individual, usually male, can be both homoerotic and heterorelational. He can enjoy his relationship with a woman while maintaining homoerotic fantasies. The possible combinations seem endless. Thus, a therapist's preset idea of what is normal for relationships, and therefore what to strive for, can be damaging to the couple seeking treatment for problems that may have little or nothing to do with their sexual feelings and behaviors.

Another example in support of the need to respect same-sex relationships as having their own set of norms and dynamics is that in heterosexual couples there continues to be considerable role differentiation in which each person assumes and takes responsibility for certain defined tasks. This is not necessarily so with same-sex couples. Both lesbian and gay male couples demonstrate significantly more role flexibility than do heterosexual couples. They respond to the multiplicity of life stresses creatively and flexibly. This is of particular interest to the relationship therapist who often struggles to develop an egalitarian relationship when working with heterosexual couples. Frequently, the heterosexual couple does not have the flexibility to manage the transition.

Also, therapists and heterosexual couples tend to place a high value on individual differentiation in therapy. When therapists strive to achieve this goal with same-sex partners, they may be less successful, since among gay and lesbian couples individuation is not as highly valued. For example, lesbian couples value high levels of cohesion more than they do differentiation, and for the most part they achieve much higher levels of closeness than do either gay males or heterosexual couples. Gay male couples, often thought of as unable to form close relationships, also achieve greater degrees of closeness than do most heterosexual couples.

There are a few guiding principles for conducting relationship therapy with gay and lesbian couples and families that honor both the complexity and the uniqueness of the relational dynamics in same-sex relationships. These principles are obviously part of therapy in general but should be particularly emphasized here.

1. Use an approach that is neutral with respect to values.
2. Examine personal attitudes and expectations for possible bias.
3. Do not assume—ask.
4. Remember that normality is culturally determined.

Case Example

When first seen, Charles was in his late 40s; his partner, Allen, was 11 years older. They had been together in a "mostly monogamous" relationship for 10 years and reported they were very much satisfied with their relationship. When they arrived in the office, they sat close together and were warm and caring with each other. When asked about their closeness, they told us that the closeness and nurturing we noticed in the office was a representative sample of their experience as a couple. Their difficulty was Allen's depression, which was severe. It had begun 6 months previously when Allen was laid off from work. His depression had been thus far refractory to treatment.

This relationship was one that challenged several stereotypes. The couple had a long-standing history of a satisfactory relationship, they were two men who were both extremely nurturing, and, in spite of their being highly enmeshed, there was no question that they were successful as a couple. The way they finished each other's sentences suggested a blurring of boundaries, a lack of differentiation; yet there was no pathology. Until Allen's depression, they were very flexible and responded creatively to most of life's curveballs.

The problem they presented to us, however, was not the depression, not the absence of sex, not the loss of income, and not the shift in roles that was the result of Allen's inability to function at home or at work. Charles was upset because Allen, a good nurturer, would not allow himself to be cared for. What had previously been a balanced relationship, with mutual giving and receiving, was now unbalanced. When Allen's difficulty in accepting nurturing was identified as the problem, he was able to talk about his early socialization, the way he took care of his mother, and his belief that in her depression she would never be able to nurture him.

The first stage of treatment involved redirecting attention from the depression to the relational/systems issue, an imbalance in the nurturing component of the relationship. In the second stage Allen changed his decision that others could or would not ever nurture him to a redecision that Charles was able and willing to nurture him and that he, Allen, was safe enough and able to allow this nurturing. The work of the third stage was accomplished outside the office as they negotiated the details of their new relationship.

Allen and Charles's relationship calls into question the whole idea of role differentiation in relational dynamics. These two were not well differentiated, and the conventional wisdom in the field characterizes low differentiation as bad and high differentiation as good. Work with gay and lesbian couples suggests this definition may not be valid.

Examining the details of a relationship such as this reminds us that the "truths" we hold dear may not be true at all. This recognition will allow us to be sensitive to the unique qualities of gays and lesbians as individuals and in the couple relationship.

■ CHILDREN AND ADOLESCENTS IN FAMILY THERAPY

One of the most common reasons for initiating family therapy is a problem with a child or children. Most frequently the problem is identified by the school, the physician, the family itself, or sometimes even the legal system. In the early days of family therapy, children's problems were most often viewed as a symptom of family dysfunction. Now, a more commonly held view is that the child's problem and the family's dysfunction are interdependent—each impacts the other.

Despite their often being the reason that family therapy is initiated, children are frequently not treated as valued individuals during the course of family therapy, regardless of the age of the child or the orientation or skill of the family therapist. When the interactional sequences in family therapy sessions are considered, it is found that a disproportionate amount of time is often spent with adults as compared with children. The result is that children generally report feeling unimportant and uninvolved. Effective family therapy requires careful attention to the needs and dictates of the children involved. In this sense, children and adolescents represent a "special population" for family therapists.

Issues for Children and Adolescents

Parents seek help with or for their child in the hope of obtaining welcome relief for the whole system. They often feel helpless, inadequate, and angry, thinking that their best efforts were inadequate to meet the problems of their child. An initial assessment and the subsequent treatment involve identifying how the family system has responded to the demands of the developmental tasks, which are outlined in Table 6–1. Along with health, the level of intellectual functioning, and possible neurological problems that can interfere with learning, these development tasks are the most important general issues of treatment with children and adolescents.

The issues most often affecting children and adolescents in family therapy today are those of neglect, abuse, and substance abuse. It is impossible to refer to the specific treatment of these issues in this concise guide. However, any therapist will be affected by a brief look here at some clear consequences of dysfunctional families, as well as our society's inability to care for its youth and indifference toward their fate. According to statistics released by the Children's Defense Fund, each day in the United States 3 children die from child abuse, 22 are murdered or die from gunshots, and 27 die from poverty; 202 are arrested for drug offenses, 307 for crimes of violence, and 370 for drinking or drunk driving—with a total of 5,314 children arrested for all offenses. Furthermore, 7,945 are reported abused or neglected; and 1.2 million latchkey children return to homes in which there is a gun.

TABLE 6–1. Child and adolescent development: summary

Age group	Developmental task	Cognitive reasoning	Role of the family system
Preschool (to age 7 or 8)	Developing self; lessening attachment on parent subsystem Learning by exploring their world, manipulating external objects Beginning to internalize family norms through behavior choice and delay of self gratification	Child moves from avoiding being caught and punished to seeking reward for doing the right things	Provides security through external limits and affirming care, eventually internalized as personal value Family system represents the norms of society to the developing child
Latency (ages 9 to 12)	Exercising an increasingly independent self by testing family norms against societal norms at school and with peers	Child desires to be perceived as good by family, school, peers and in his or her social network	Provides limits on amount of time away from home, balancing system dependence and extended limits for the process of individuation
Early adolescence (puberty to age 15)	Resolving increased demand from personal responsibility at home, at school, and in personal relationships Developing self-esteem by comparing self to others	Adolescent desires to have social standards reflected in his or her personal identity Standards are based on the adolescent's social or cultural allegiance	Physical and emotional support provides limits for the adolescent to explore new roles, thought, and emotion associated to his or her emergence into the adult world

TABLE 6–1. **Child and adolescent development: summary** *(continued)*

Age group	Developmental task	Cognitive reasoning	Role of the family system
Late adolescence (ages 15 to 20)	Assuming personal responsibility balanced with acceptance of freedoms and privileges in all aspects of life and relationships Using their own life decisions as a measure of success	Society must live by rules, and those rules must be fair The rules become internalized to engage in the give and take of society	Adjusts the systems rules, roles, and boundaries that allow the adolescent to make commitments and decisions and to choose life directions, making allowance for success and failure

Treatment Focus

One of the important tasks in the initial meeting with a family is *making contact*. More than just saying hello, making contact with—engaging or joining with—a child means that the therapist recognizes the developmental and cognitive level of the child and designs the conversation to meet the child's particular needs. With the young child, this usually means engaging in some form of family play that will allow the child and the family to use the material gained for entrance into the family system. With older children and adolescents, recognition of their growing autonomy and need for confidentiality becomes more important.

Involving the family in a large drawing project with ambiguous directions allows the therapist to watch how parents and children relate to each other, how they engage or keep each other separate, how they maintain or cross generational and individual boundaries, and how they help or hinder each other. Asking the older child to construct a living tableau of the family as he or she sees it is another example of engaging the child in a way that is consistent with his or her developmental level. This activity supports an independent view of the family and provides an opportunity for the therapist to observe how the family manages different views.

Although children usually want to be part of the treatment process, they do not want to be the sole focus of treatment. They get more out of treatment when the therapist is able to communicate at their level and be a person to whom they can relate. Adolescents, on the other hand, are more concerned about how others perceive them, particularly with regard to their being in therapy.

Therapists working with adolescents often encounter early resistance. To a large degree such resistance is appropriate, because adolescents are reluctant to give their trust to a therapist unless they have reason to believe that the therapist is capable, will not be overwhelmed by the family, and will not identify the adolescent as the sole source of the problem. Adolescents particularly enjoy being involved with expressive techniques such as family sculpting, communication-skills learning, and dance or drama.

Confidentiality is a very important factor in working with families. It is a difficult issue for parents, children, and adolescents, but even more so for therapists, who may espouse the cause of openness but frequently run into requests to meet individually and to not tell parents about certain difficulties and escapades. The position that we take is that our job is not to be tattletales but to help any individual talk to the others in the relationship unit. (As an aside, confidentiality is, of course, also an enormous problem when working with couples, and it can be handled in the same general way.)

Therapy that focuses on family systems and integrates elements of play therapy approaches is specifically suited to treating families with children. Play sessions need not be limited to the office, but can be extended outside the area for nondisrupted interaction. Again, the activities must be age-appropriate so that all members can participate. Parents find this form of therapy useful too, because they can relate to their child's play from the perspective of their own family history. Having a family member make up a new game with its own set of rules can be informative about the flexibility or rigidity of the family system.

Case Example

The Minton family consisted of mother, Ginnie (age 33); father, Marv (age 33); and their son, Howard (age 6). The family was referred by the school because Howard was getting into fights with other children. In the first family meeting Howard rejected all attempts on the part of any of the adults in the room to make contact with him. His parents responded to his negativism and oppositional behavior by talking around and above him. The resulting picture was of two adults talking about Howard, who was out of the picture except for occasional outbursts in which he would walk over and punch either of his parents. After chastising him, they went back to their discussion.

The first-stage intervention with this family was designed to make contact with all three people, to help them make contact with one another, and to acquire more information about how the system maintained the problem. Several options for intervening into the system were available. We chose to note that neither Marv nor Ginnie was aware of Howard's depression, each being wedded to their own view of reality and their own narratives about what was happening with their son.

We asked all three of the Mintons to draw a picture of how they viewed their family and then to talk about the picture. Ginnie's picture showed a close-knit family, whereas Marv's revealed a portrait with each of the people equal and equidistant from one another. Howard drew his parents talking to each other, depicting himself as a black circle far away. Since Howard was actively engaged in this process, we were able to encourage them to work together on a joint picture of the family. The parents continued to pay little attention to Howard. They failed to include him in the process or to validate his contribution to the effort. In fact, most of the verbal interaction centered around telling Howard what not to do.

Not seeing—not noticing—was labeled as the dominant metaphor for the family. This was the main systems issue we all agreed to change. Once this step was taken it was easy to move to the work of Stage II and to determine the origins of Marv's distancing, Ginny's difficulties with seeing problems, and Howard's depression. Ultimately Howard responded well to a combination of medication, changes in his parents, and their new approach to him.

■ RECONSTITUTED FAMILIES

Reconstituted families—also known as remarried families or stepfamilies—are a fact of today's life. Approximately 3,000 children per day see their parents divorce, and 3,500 babies per day are born to unmarried women. By the year 2000 nearly half the population of the United States will be part of a reconstituted family. This astounding number should alert therapists to the necessity of understanding the reconstituted family and the issues its members face.

Issues for Reconstituted Families

Practical issues play an extremely significant role in this population group. Although there are no studies that allow us to rank-order or otherwise prioritize these issues, a nonexhaustive list points out the daunting tasks that face step- or "blended" families.

Economic issues are extremely important. It is well known that most single mothers face reduced socioeconomic status as a consequence of divorce, whereas most divorced men actually experience an increase in their socioeconomic status and functioning. (The widespread occurrence of the "deadbeat dad" syndrome is also well observed.) This lowered standard of living presents a problem for children who live primarily with their mothers; many tend to drop out of school prematurely, become sexually active prematurely, and marry prematurely. Moreover, these all-to-frequent consequences of divorce are of particular significance to girls.

When single mothers remarry or enter into a committed relationship with a live-in partner, the family configurations that ensue from these reconstituted families are as complex and variable as the number of families themselves. There can be full, half, or stepsiblings, and perhaps even adopted or foster siblings as well. Perhaps, too, the other parent has similarly remarried. Confusion, acting out, depression, rivalries, favoritism, manipulation, coalitions, antipathy, rebellion, and other problems that frequent first-time families are considerably amplified in the reconstituted family; consequently, the everyday problems of family life are also amplified.

Reconstituted families have less control of their own family life than when the original family was intact. Because the children of divorced parents often move back and forth between households, a crisis generated in one household can have a major impact on the other household. In addition, this movement reactivates the everpresent, if underlying, issue of loss. Each visit to the "other" parent has the potential to reawaken feelings of loss that resulted from the parents' decision to go separate ways; these feelings are compounded by resentment, anger, and even an irrational sense of guilt over possibly having caused the rupture itself. The abiding loss affects both children and parents, although parents—particularly those who have formed new relationships—tend to focus on the children's loss rather than their own.

There is also evidence that over time the out-of-home parent, usually the father, decreases contact with the children and that this contributes to their sense of loss. Though this distancing, or even disappearance, is more likely to happen with less-educated fathers, it is nonetheless a problem in all socioeconomic classes.

Treatment Focus

Divorce, single parenting, and remarriage are life events with a high potential for pain that needs to be resolved. Reparative factors that allow people to go on to make satisfactory adjustments include the following:

- Acceptance of the loss and the appropriate grieving
- Tolerance of the ambiguity in the living and the relationship situations
- The ability to maintain object constancy
- The acceptance of their family constellation and living situation as healthy even though their situation may not be typical

Treatment needs to consider all these issues.

Therapists face a large problem when working with reconstituted families: the definition of normality. Parents and children feel misunderstood when they believe that their therapist is working from an ideal rather than a reality-based model. If we, as therapists, use the traditional one-marriage, two-parent family as the standard of reference for normality, we run the risk of failing to recognize the particular struggles and needs of the reconstituted family. The bonds that are formed in reconstituted families are necessarily different from the bonds formed by children to their biologic parents in an attachment that begins at birth. In many such families, parents attempt to achieve normality by behaving as if they were the child's only parents, thus expecting and even demanding the child's undivided loyalty. This is a difficult course to take, particularly if the child is old enough to have a clear memory of the absent parent.

It is crucial for all parents in a reconstituted family, including those who are not legally married, to recognize the reality of their situation and to develop family relationships based on this reality. Parents must accept and allow for flexible boundaries that accommodate the child's other parent. The reconstituted family is no better or worse—only different. If therapists attempt to guide (consciously or not) the stepfamily toward a model that does not include the former partners and coparents, they may be setting an unrealistic goal—and in the process setting the family up for defeat.

Other important treatment interventions include the development of new family rituals. It is hard to organize special weekend time when the children are in another house every other weekend. Yet this type of constancy is exactly what is needed to maintain the idea of family and the security and predictability it implies. It behooves the family therapist to help each reconstituted family develop its own new rituals.

Case Example

Marty Johnson and his new wife, Janet, came into therapy because Janet and Marty's son Arnold were continually at war with each other. From its start, only months earlier, the new marriage had a stormy history. When he and Janet met, Marty had been divorced for 6 years; for most of that time he was engaged in a bitter custody battle with his ex-wife, who he declared was emotionally unstable. Marty and Janet entered treatment just at the point that Marty had been granted primary custody of his two children, Arnold (age 12) and Maya (age 10). The intensity of the battle between stepmother and stepson had increased almost in parallel with the custody battle. Whenever a fight occurred between his new wife and son, Marty attempted to mediate the battle, and this left both Janet and Arnold feeling unsupported.

The couple faced additional difficulties. Janet resented Marty's obligation to provide spousal support. Within a short time a new baby would need to be integrated into this reconstituted family. Moreover, religious differences needed to be taken into account. The sibling rivalry between Arnold and Maya, as well as the markedly different personality styles of the family members, brought further stress. An additional concern was that Arnold was becoming more socially isolated.

This complex situation illustrates some of the most important aspects of treating reconstituted families. Although they were in a new family, Arnold and Maya were in fact part of three separate units: one with their biological mother, one with their father, and one with the new family, including a stepmother and a soon-arriving half sibling. Not surprisingly, they had torn loyalties. The bitterness of the divorce and the prolonged custody battle prevented any grieving. Their loyalty to their mother interfered with their ability to form an attachment to the new family.

Understandably, Janet felt left out—and she was, in fact, kept out. Her own history made it particularly difficult for her to tolerate this exclusion and further thrust her into the role of the outsider, a role already too familiar to her. Marty's intense connection with his son also contributed to the problem. In his anger at his ex-wife, he too had never grieved his loss and therefore was unable to engage fully in his new marriage.

In our experience, reconstituted families often enter treatment in a state of crisis, just as Marty and Janet had done. The treatment plan begins with creating a safe environment with a focus on diffusing the conflict as quickly as possible. The grieving process over past losses can then be completed, and the issue of divided loyalties can be explored and, hopefully, resolved.

Because events that occur in one family have an impact on the other family, the reconstituted family often needs to learn new joint problem-solving techniques. In the Johnsons' case, it was particularly important to focus on the problem-solving process rather than on the problem itself. Thus, when Arnold arrived home in a surly mood after a visit to his biological mother, the question for his father and stepmother became, "How can the two of us help Arnold manage his feelings about his mother and the need to leave her?" This systemic or first-stage intervention, by helping to refocus the therapy on the marital dialogue and parenting plan, consequently took the heat off the stepmother-stepson relationship, thus preventing further labeling of Arnold as the problem. All too frequently children who are defiant are seen as the identified patient, whereas it is the family itself that needs treatment.

Although the above question was framed in the context of the family therapy setting, the work was actually done in couple therapy. This is often the case with reconstituted families, particularly those in which the children are too young to be involved or the feelings expressed are too intense for children to be exposed to them. Even when the children are not physically present, however, it is always important to be *thinking family*.

The work of Stage II in the Johnson family was complicated. Arnold, the lightning rod for his family, could not grieve the loss of his biologic family as long as Marty, whom Arnold adored, was so angry at Arnold's mother. Until Arnold resolved his loyalty issues, he could not allow himself to connect with his stepmother. Janet was not helping the process of grieving because she could not tolerate Arnold's "coldness" toward her.

Stage II work involved addressing each of these issues individually. In Stage III, attention was focused on the present, with Marty and Janet developing and then rehearsing ways to deal with difficult situations (the visits to the mother) as well as new problem-solving strategies.

■ **FAMILIES WITH SUBSTANCE ABUSE**

When 18 million adults have a problem with alcohol and 14 million have a problem with other mind- and behavior-affecting substances, it is hard to imagine a family that has not been touched by substance abuse. Thus, this widespread disorder should be of special concern to relationship therapists.

Issues for Families With Substance Abuse

Substance abuse (of drugs and/or alcohol) creates disruption for families through financial strain, loss of jobs, legal problems, association with various forms of violent and criminal behavior, and interference with interpersonal relationships. Consider this: every 15 seconds in the United States some form of domestic violence is committed against a spouse or significant other, and a majority of the perpetrators are under the influence of drugs or alcohol, or both.

For some years family difficulties were generally thought to be at the root of substance use disorders. Thus, therapists wondered about the impact of the "codependent" partner on the abuser, for a long time adhering to the stereotypical picture of the husband drinking to escape his shrewish wife. More recently, the biopsychosocial model of substance abuse has become the dominant paradigm. In this model substance abuse is treated as a medical problem, and a reciprocal relationship is posited between the disorder, the person using, and his or her family. This relatively new way of conceptualizing problems of substance abuse in the family context has resulted in entirely new approaches to the disorder.

Treatment Focus

We no longer think of treating alcoholism with MFT approaches. Instead, we think of using MFT to motivate the index patient to enter an active treatment program that focuses on the disease and on the emotional needs of the substance abuser. We also think of MFT as being helpful in the aftercare program, or maintenance phase, of the overall treatment program. Finally, we have moved from thinking of termination to recognizing that substance abuse is a lifelong problem that requires continual attention, as may the family and couple relationships of the substance-abusing person.

Several models use staged intervention for the treatment of substance abuse. Typically, the resources of the entire family are used to simultaneously confront and support the abusing person. The goal of this confrontation is to help the substance abuser get to the point that he or she will enter a primary treatment program. Treatment programs generally focus on the needs of the individual and address the entire biopsychosocial spectrum. After treatment, the patient in the last stage of all models returns to his or her family, and issues related to maintenance are given attention.

Marital and family therapy is not as effective in treating drug use disorders as it is in treating alcoholism. In families affected by drug abuse, the abusing person generally becomes the central focus of the family's life. Many normal family functions stop; a helplessness pervades the family as everything they try fails. In this regard, treatment with drug abusers and their families is similar to treatment with families in which one person has a severe chronic illness. Typically, persons who abuse drugs are younger than individuals with alcoholism, although young persons with alcoholism also are more difficult to treat. This factor, a younger age, may in some way account for poorer treatment outcomes.

As with patients with schizophrenia, the family dynamics of substance abusers' current family as well as their family of origin influence the rate of patient relapse. Perhaps the mechanism of action is also the same in both populations. In families with schizophrenic members, high levels of expressed emotion are associated with relapse; therefore, relationship therapy is targeted toward altering this dynamic. Unfortunately, no data are available to clarify the mechanism of action of the psychotherapeutic process in substance use disorders. But obviously it behooves relationship therapists to consider what we already know from work with families with patients with schizophrenia in order to determine the value of extrapolating this experience to treatment of substance abusers.

Case Example

Jill (age 51) was referred by her internist for treatment of anxiety. During the course of her treatment Jill revealed the extent of her husband's drinking problem. His drinking was seriously impairing their relationship and was beginning to affect his work life and jeopardize his health as well. Robert (age 52) came into a conjoint session and readily admitted to drinking, even to being an alcoholic. Referring back to a period 10 years earlier when he had been abstinent for 6 months, he insisted he could not tolerate how he felt when he was not drinking and described being immobilized by anxiety and depression.

Jill and Robert's situation continued unabated for almost another year. During that time Jill focused on developing her own strengths and finding new ways to deal with Robert. She regularly attended Al-Anon meetings. Finally, when Jill felt strong enough, she was able to involve the entire family in family therapy. The family meetings were emotional sessions during which the family history of alcoholism was outlined; two of the couple's four adult children revealed their own struggles to control their drinking.

After several family meetings, Robert agreed to enter a residential treatment program based on the AA model. This change in willingness to get treatment occurred only with the reassurance of help to actively treat any residual depression and anxiety when he returned home. At the same time that Robert made his decision, two of his children joined Alcoholics Anonymous (AA), and the entire family became involved with Al-Anon. Posthospital therapy focused on the couple's relationship, managing Robert's anxiety and depression, and supporting his continued involvement with AA. Jill also continued in her own individual therapy.

This vignette illustrates a typical way family therapy approaches substance use disorders. Family therapy in this context is used primarily to motivate people toward individual therapy and to reduce the stressors that make maintenance difficult. Most approaches to the treatment of substance use disorders have a significant psychoeducational component. Many, if not most, make use of community resources such as AA and other "12 Step" programs.

■ FAMILIES WITH CHRONIC ILLNESS

Patients with chronic illness, almost without regard to the specific illness, present a special challenge to the family therapist. Often an illness or injury is sufficiently disabling and the ramifications so far-reaching that the illness becomes both the central fact and the organizing factor of a family's life. As the disability becomes chronic, feelings of resentment and helplessness follow, along with those of inadequacy and failure. Both individual and family emotional and energy resources are severely strained, and a sense of hopelessness about the future sets in.

The history of how chronic illness is conceptualized sheds an interesting light on present-day thinking. For many years the psychosomatic model dominated the field. Certain illnesses—including duodenal ulcer, rheumatoid arthritis, and hypertension, among others—were regarded as the body's response to intrapersonal conflict. It was thought that conflict produces an emotional response, ranging from anxiety to anger, that when turned against the self causes tissue damage or disease.

Later, a distinction was made between disease and illness. Disease became the diagnosable medical problem (e.g., arthritis, cancer, depression), and illness became the patient's subjective response to the disease, including not only pain and suffering but also acceptance or nonacceptance of the sick role.

The next iteration of theories of chronic illness recognized the family's impact on the patient with the disease. As mentioned in Chapter 2, the realization that the family's behavior and attitude could have a significant effect on an individual's well-being led directly to the development of family therapy.

More recently, therapists have recognized that the relationship between a sick person and his or her family is a two-way street, with each side affecting the other in a reciprocal fashion. It was also discovered that changes in the interactional patterns between the sick person and the family could result in improvements in the quality of life for the family, a reduction in relapse rates, and reduced morbidity and mortality.

Issues for Families With Chronic Illness

When chronic illness invades a family, the illness becomes the central fact of life for the family. Often a financial burden exists, and always a time and energy drain occurs that results from taking care of the personal needs of the disabled person. Changes take place in a host of family rituals and patterns, such as mealtimes, entertainment opportunities, activities, and sleep-wake cycles.

In addition, the family must accommodate many complicated, ambivalent emotional responses, not only to the disabled person but also to the changed family situation. Understanding and caring coexist with resentment, anger, and withdrawal. The family's view of itself—the story it tells itself to achieve a cohesive identity— changes drastically. For instance, a narrative formerly describing the family as being much involved with their children's athletic activities might now shift to a family narrative concerned primarily with dad's heart problems. As the illness endures, the new story becomes more fixed.

Treatment Focus

Based on current understanding of the problem of chronic illness, the goal of a family intervention is to alter the interactional pattern *within* the family. This statement contains a subtle change from the historical position, for now the focus is no longer on altering the interactional pattern *between* the family and the patient. Family interventions in the context of chronic illness do best when they approach the family from a dual perspective: the extent to which the family has reorganized itself around the illness, and the degree of individuation (actual or needed) of the family members.

The burden experienced by individual family members is related to the degree of individuation achieved by each person. The more secure family members are within themselves, the less threatened they are by the illness of one of their members, and, hence, the less apt they are to take personally the problems of adjusting to the realities of another person's chronic illness.

For families at the upper end of the continuum of individuation, the psychoeducational approaches are very useful. These interventions, which may or may not be carried out by trained therapists, provide information to the family about the illness, guidance on available medical and social resources in the community, and access to group support when needed. As the illness becomes more chronic and the family's resources and coping skills are more taxed, even healthy families tend to seek group support. Educational approaches can also be an important adjunct in working with families with a recent onset of illness.

For families at the lower end of the continuum of individuation, family therapy is specifically indicated. Unfortunately, it is not clear whether insight-oriented MFT or behavioral MFT works best. It also is not clear whether therapy that focuses on the system or therapy that focuses on the individual affords better results.

Case Example

When they met each other at work, Marla and Herb were 23 and 25 years old, respectively. Energetic, outgoing people with an active social life, they were passionate about outdoor activities, particularly jogging and hiking. They dated for 3 years and then married.

During the second year of marriage, Marla was in an auto accident and sustained back injuries that ultimately required a total of five surgeries. After 2 years of being incapacitated, she was able to resume some physical activities. However, she still suffered from severe pain resulting from an unusual complication of surgical procedures—scar formation around the nerves to the lower half of her body.

The couple's personal life was thrown into a turmoil. They had to put their plans to have a family on hold. Since Marla could not sit long enough to travel even a short distance by car, it was impossible for her to hold a job. Consequently, the family finances became strained. Roughly half of Marla's waking time was involved in rehabilitation/physical therapy and medical appointments; the rest of her time was spent recovering from those activities. Severely depressed, she often thought of suicide.

Meanwhile, Herb, who had initially been very supportive, became resentful and withdrawn. He began to spend more time with his friends, acting more and more like a single man. Although he denied having extramarital relations, he continually complained to Marla and his friends about the lack of sex.

When we first saw this couple, 5 years after the accident, all of their dialogue focused on some aspect of Marla's disability or care. Meeting all of the criteria for having a severely disturbed couple relationship, they were beyond benefit from a purely educational intervention. The defining factor of the Stage I intervention (see Chapter 4) was helping them rewrite their story.

We began by encouraging them to tell their own personal stories, including their hopes and dreams for themselves and their relationship. Conjointly we began to talk of Marla's condition as not residing within Marla, but as something apart from her. Marla's condition became an object, a problem for the two of them to deal with. We then began to help them develop a new story.

Neither Herb nor Marla was particularly well established as an individual in his or her own right. Marla, the youngest child in her family of origin, had been a high school prom queen. Admired by everyone, her beauty and athleticism were essential parts of her identity. Fortunately, she realized she had other strengths as well, and she ultimately decided to include and develop these as part of her new identity. Herb's story was similar. His identity was tied up in his physical activity. The perennial adolescent, he was uncertain about his interest and suitability as a family man.

In Stage II of RRTM these individual issues were taken up during couple-therapy sessions. As part of this work, Marla and Herb decided to start their family. This, of course, was done in consultation with Marla's physicians, who thoughtfully assessed her limitations in the context of carrying, bearing, and raising children. In Stage III the couple addressed the practical realities of their redecisions and their new narrative.

■ FAMILIES WITH ELDERLY MEMBERS

A commercial, recently featured on television, depicts a toddler struggling to get to the top of a long, wide flight of steps; at the same time, a somewhat frail, elderly man is very carefully working his way down. As they meet in the middle and sit down, the caption unfolds: "They have a lot in common."

Family therapy with families in which one of the members is elderly has a lot in common with family therapy with families with young children. To fully appreciate those commonalities, it is useful to review the life cycle from the family perspective.

Children begin life physically and emotionally dependent. It is their task to learn to think and care for themselves, and eventually to start their own families. It is their parents' task to help them to thereby become independent people. At the beginning of the life cycle, boundaries are clear: parents are parents, and children are children. Each generational group within the family has its own skills, roles, obligations, and responsibilities. As children grow older, it becomes more difficult to maintain boundaries. As they grow older, children normally want to become more independent, with some beginning to take charge of their own lives before their parents think they are ready to do so. However, some parents, because of illness, misfortune, or personal difficulties, are incapable of fulfilling their part of the bargain, so they allow or encourage the children virtually to assume the parental role in terms of responsibility and even authority. At some point, most offspring establish themselves successfully in their own lives, and for a time, at least, there is some physical and emotional separation between the generations.

Issues for Families With Elderly Members

The period of later life presents new challenges. Inevitably, when parents grow aged, they become less able to take care of themselves. Sometimes the problem is financial, but often it is chronic illness. And as people live increasingly longer, disabling dementias are apt to occur. Regardless of the cause, the parent-child relationship is changed, and these changes stir up old interpersonal conflicts as well as personal doubts.

As noted above, therapy with a family that has an elderly member in some ways resembles therapy with a family that has a young child. The focus may vary between the two: in family therapy with a child, attention is paid in particular to the child's developmental needs, whereas in family therapy with an aging adult, disability and dependency issues are usually addressed. In both situations, however, the therapist must work at managing the boundaries and keeping the generations separate.

It is relevant for therapists to recognize the enormity of the problem of parents' aging that confronts our society and to understand how it already impacts, and will increasingly impact, the family system. Demographers anticipate that by the year 2030, 21.8% of the United States population will be over 65. This statistic is particularly important with respect to families, because with increasing life expectancy and the tendency to have smaller families, existing families will become numerically dominated by older members. With aging comes the likely issue of decreasing physical capacity, which translates into a decreased ability to care for oneself.

Estimates vary, but it is believed that as many as 60% of the adult population alive today will require nursing home care at some point in their lives. Before these individuals enter a nursing home, most of the care will be provided by family members. In many situations this care involves either living with a parent or parents in their own home or taking them into one's own family home, where dependent children—the third generation—may also be living. Currently, most family caregivers are women (72%), with a large proportion over 50 years of age (38%). Moreover, the majority of these caregivers are now fully employed (52%) and also have children under age 18 living at home.

Other changes in the structure of families will also impact the provision of care for elderly family members. Our society has become more mobile: people change jobs and relocate more frequently and farther away from the family of origin's home base. The divorce and remarriage rates are higher, both for younger and older people. A result of these important changes is that the ties between family members—the loyalty bonds that hold families together—are both more complicated and more complex. It is also probable that in most situations the primary responsibility for caring for the older generations (parents and possibly grandparents as well) cannot be readily shared among a group of siblings and other close relatives, as happened in extended families in the past.

When an adult child is caring for an aging parent or parents, family life is affected enormously. The problems occur at several levels and in different dimensions. The adult child usually has several major responsibilities, so he or she, as well as the rest of the family, experiences conflict about which to fulfill first. The caregiver is apt to feel torn by competing loyalties. There is also the disappointment that just when life is supposed to be getting simpler, with children growing up and "leaving the nest," it becomes more complicated, with burdensome new responsibilities. Furthermore, the family must handle the ever-present issue of the eventual death of the parent or grandparent. All of these issues, separately and together, can have a profound impact on the caregiver and her (usually her) family.

The reversal of parent-child roles also poses a potential problem, with both the adult child and the aging parent feeling uncomfortable in their new roles. Ambivalence is especially present when the disabled adult does not graciously or gratefully accept the dependency that goes along with the age- or illness-related disability. Even if parents and children can readily accept new roles, other important concerns crop up. Since many of society's traditional family caregivers—the female members—now have outside work commitments, the extra strain of caring for a disabled parent can be especially significant. The time-consuming tasks of chauffeuring and providing social contacts and entertainment for the elderly family member can be difficult to add to the other activities in managing a household.

Moreover, there is often a financial burden that goes beyond the issue of added responsibility. It costs more to feed, house, and clothe the aging parent, and medical expenses may not be adequately reimbursed. These costs do not begin to address the cost of additional nursing and respite care when needed. The health problems also go beyond age and physical disability. Alcoholism occurs in 10% to 15% of the population over age 65 and can be very difficult to diagnose. Depression occurs in another 10% to 15%. Even though there is some overlap between these two groups, the figures are impressive.

Caring for an aging parent or parents can involve addressing problems whose resolution requires time-consuming, frustrating contacts with government agencies (e.g., Social Security, Medicare, IRS) as well as with the legal system.

Finally, some issues arise that are, for the most part, new to this generation of older people. The family must provide protection to reduce vulnerability to the growing number of scams that take advantage of the elderly, less mobile person, who may be gullible and incapable of rational self-protection. People robbed of their financial base will, of necessity, depend further on their children and other relatives for different forms of assistance. Elderly family members are also more likely to remarry or cohabit than in past years, and this brings new relational and potential legal problems into the picture. Not always are their choices in companionship pleasing to their adult children.

Treatment Focus

Working with the elderly requires an understanding of the medical, psychological, psychiatric, and social problems that face them and their families, as well as those problems that are specific to each individual and his or her family. For instance, it is comparatively straightforward to treat alcoholism in the elderly when the focus is on the stress of aging and the coexisting depression, and when therapy is in the context of a supportive environment. It is similarly straightforward to treat depression in the elderly as long as we first make the appropriate diagnosis. It is not yet possible to effectively treat dementia of the Alzheimer's type by slowing or reversing its relentless course, but it is possible to offer significant help. (Some other forms of dementia may be addressed through drug therapy or nutritional medicine.) Again, the first step is diagnosis.

The situation of family therapy with families with aging members, in which the initial focus is on the individual, is different from the more traditional MFT situation, in which the initial focus is on the relationship. It is similar, however, to the situation of family therapy with young children, in which the focus is necessarily on the developmental needs of the child. Similarly, when there is a chronic illness, we attend to the medical needs before we address the system.

The relational aspects of the parent-child interaction are important, since more often than not one of the children will assume or be assigned the caregiver role. Acceptance and performance of this role appears to be directly related to the degree to which that child has already been successful at becoming autonomous. Failure of individuation results in a high sense of perceived burden. In addition, problems frequently arise between siblings, with resentments being felt on each side. Caregivers often become angry because they do not receive adequate help, and noncaregivers may be concerned about being left out of decisions, including the management of resources that they expect someday will belong in part to them. Also important are, as mentioned earlier, the issues related to the caregiver's current family and the competing loyalties.

One model often used for working with families with elderly members utilizes a multifaceted systems approach. The family system is assessed with respect to the attachment/caregiving dimension, openness of communication, and problem-solving ability. This information is factored in with a multidimensional assessment of individual strengths or resilience, genetically endowed or learned vulnerabilities, health-enhancing individual and family factors, and indicators that suggest high risk. Interventions range from consultation, which is primarily psychoeducational, to more traditional interventions, which are aimed at promoting clear boundaries and developing strong attachments.

Case Example

Margaret (age 72) was referred by her physician because she was becoming combative at home. Her husband, Bob (age 76), came into the office with her. Margaret had numerous medical problems, the most relevant of which was cerebrovascular disease, which had resulted in several small strokes that caused progressive loss of memory. Her mental condition had deteriorated significantly in the past 6 months. She was neatly dressed and her affect was pleasant, but her memory loss was profound and she confabulated when challenged. She was unaware of cognitive difficulties and of how difficult it was to take care of her.

Since Margaret could not be left alone, Bob, who had gone back to work after retirement, had enlisted the help of their adult daughter in caregiving. Jennifer and her husband had sold their home and moved into her parents' house, the family home. Husband, daughter, and son-in-law were simultaneously committed to caring for Margaret—and all of them were feeling angry about it.

Following the model of RRT as applied to work with the elderly, we attended to the individual assessment and then moved to Stage I and subsequently to Stage III.

First, we clarified the diagnosis with the family, who had been hoping a cure for Margaret's disease would be found. Then, we determined that the medications were not helping, and they were stopped. These first two steps were taken in consultation with the family physician.

Next, within Stage I, we addressed the high level of over-involvement that all four family members had with each other. We pointed out that the entire focus of the family's life had become caring for Margaret. In addition, we also sought to understand and frame the family's caretaking activities in terms of the self-sacrifice involved. In this context we reviewed the individual life histories from the transgenerational perspective and helped each of the participants focus on his or her own life goals.

We learned that Bob was currently overseeing the care of his own aged mother as well; she was in a nursing home suffering from dementia of the Alzheimer's type. Bob was having difficulty accepting that his mother no longer recognized him, or anyone. We also learned that Jennifer had stepped in in order to rescue her father as much as to care for her mother, reaffirming the transgenerational pattern of fulfilling obligations.

Jennifer's helping her parents was threatening her own marriage, and she was also having trouble maintaining a job. In a sense, she was in the process of sacrificing her own life. In the work that was done in therapy, Jennifer clarified what she wanted for her life. Bob observed how his daughter was taking his place, and he decided to take charge again of his wife's care. He recognized his own conflict: he could not work and care for his wife at the same time. Although he was not sure how he would resolve this dilemma, he knew he could not allow his daughter to sacrifice her own goals. His personal work was done with Jennifer in the room. Bob reconsidered his relationship with his wife in the light of his attachment to his mother, and this realignment freed Jennifer to lead her own life.

The focus in Stage III was on flushing out the practical details of managing Margaret's disability in a way that was congruent with Bob's values and beliefs.

Working with families with elderly members is one of the most challenging ventures for the family therapist. The issues are complicated, some are unsolvable, and the stakes are high. It is difficult work for therapists also because it awakens concerns about our own mortality and about our relationships with our parents.

■ READINGS

Marital and Sex Therapy

American Psychiatric Association: Diagnostic and Statistical Manual of Mental Disorders, 4th Edition. Washington, DC, American Psychiatric Association, 1994

Bader E, Pearson P: In Quest of the Mythical Mate. New York, Brunner/Mazel, 1988

Gottman J: Why Marriages Succeed or Fail. New York, Simon & Schuster, 1994

Hendrix H: Getting the Love You Want. New York, Henry Holt, 1988

Jacobson N, Margolin G: Marital Therapy: Strategies Based on Social Learning and Behavior Exchange Principles. New York, Brunner/Mazel, 1979

Kaplan H: The Evaluation of Sexual Disorders: Psychological and Medical Aspects. New York, Brunner/Mazel, 1983

Mason M: Family therapy as the emerging context for sex therapy, in Handbook of Family Therapy. Edited by Gurman AS, Kniskern DP. New York, Brunner/Mazel, 1991, pp 478–507

Schnarch D: Constructing the Sexual Crucible: An Integration of Sexual and Marital Therapy. New York, WW Norton, 1991

Gay and Lesbian Families

Green R, Bettinger M, Zacks E: Are lesbian couples fused and gay male couples disengaged?: questioning gender straightjackets, in Lesbians and Gays in Couples and Families: A Handbook for Therapists. Edited by Laird J, Green R. San Francisco, CA, Jossey-Bass, 1996, pp 185–230

Krestan J: Lesbian daughters and lesbian mother: the crisis of disclosure from a family systems perspective. Journal of Psychotherapy and the Family 3:113–130, 1987

Morales R: Ethnic minority families and minority gays and lesbians, in Homosexuality and Family Relations. Edited by Bozett F, Sussman M. Binghamton, NY, Haworth, 1990, pp 217–239

Children and Adolescents in Family Therapy

Allen J, Allen B: Working with children and adolescents, in Redecision Therapy: A Brief Action Oriented Approach. Edited by Lennox C. Northvale, NJ, Jason Aronson, 1997, pp 227–254

Downey G, Coyne J: Children of depressed parents: an integrative review. Psychol Bull 108:50–76, 1990

Focht L, Beardslee W: Speech after long silence: the uses of narrative therapy in a preventive intervention for children of parents with affective disorder. Fam Process 35:407–422, 1997

Moltz D: Bipolar disorder and the family: an integrative model. Fam Process 32:409–423, 1993

Oaklander V: Windows to Our Children. Moab, UT, Real People Press, 1978

Reconstituted Families

Bray J: Systems oriented therapy with stepfamilies, in Integrating Family Therapy: Handbook of Family Psychology and Systems Theory. Edited by Mikesell R, Lusterman D, McDaniel S. Washington, DC, American Psychological Association, 1995, pp 141–160

Visher E, Visher J: Therapy With Stepfamilies. New York, Brunner/Mazel, 1996

Wallerstein J, Blakeslee S: Second Chances: Men, Women and Children, a Decade After Divorce. New York, Ticknor & Fields, 1989

Walsh F: Promoting healthy functioning in divorced and remarried families, in Handbook of Family Therapy, Vol II. Edited by Gurman AS, Kniskern DP. New York, Brunner/Mazel, 1991, pp 525–545

Families With Substance Abuse

Edwards M, Steinglass P: Family therapy treatment outcomes for alcoholism. Journal of Marital and Family Therapy 21:475–510, 1995

Liddle H, Dakof G: The efficacy of family therapy for drug abuse: promising but not definitive. Journal of Marital and Family Therapy 21:511–544, 1995

O'Farell T, Choquette K, et al: Behavioral marital therapy with and without relapse prevention sessions for alcoholics and their wives. J Stud Alcohol 54:652–666, 1993

Stanton M: Family treatment approaches to drug abuse problems: a review. Fam Process 18:251–280, 1979

Families With Chronic Illness

Campbell T, Patterson J: The effectiveness of family interventions in the treatment of physical illness. Journal of Marital and Family Therapy 21:545–584, 1995

Gonzalez S, Steinglass P, Reiss D: Family centered interventions for the chronically disabled: eight-session multiple-family discussion group program [treatment manual]. Washington, DC, George Washington University Rehabilitation Research and Training Center, 1986

Leahey M, Wright L: Intervening in families with chronic illness. Family Systems Medicine 3:60–69, 1985

Perlmutter R: A Family Approach to Psychiatric Disorders. Washington, DC, American Psychiatric Press, 1996, pp 159–182

Rolland J: In sickness and in health: the impact of illness on couple's relationship. Journal of Marital and Family Therapy 20:327–347, 1994

Serrano J: Working with chronically disabled children's families: a biopsychosocial approach. Child and Adolescent Mental Health Care 3:57–168, 1993

Wynne L, Shields C, Sirkin M: Illness, family theory and family therapy, I: conceptual issues. Fam Process 31:3–18, 1992

Families With Elderly Members

Adamson D, Feinauer L, Lund D, et al: Factors affecting marital happiness of caregivers of the elderly in multigenerational families. American Journal of Family Therapy 20:62–70, 1992

DeGenova M: Elderly life review therapy: a Bowen approach. American Journal of Family Therapy 19:160–166, 1991

Draper B, Anstey K: Psychosocial stressors, physical illness and the spectrum of depression in elderly inpatients. Aust N Z J Psychiatry 30:567–572, 1996

Hughston D, Hughston G: Legal ramifications of elderly cohabitation: necessity for recognition of its implications by family psychotherapists. Journal of Psychotherapy and the Family 5:163–172, 1989

Johnson J: Risk factors associated with negative interactions between family caregivers and elderly care–receivers. Int J Aging Hum Dev 43:7–20, 1996

Peterson M, Zimberg S: Treating alcoholism: an age-specific intervention that works for older patients. Geriatrics 51:45–49, 1996

Rabin C, Bressler Y, Prager E: Caregiver burden and personal autonomy: differentiation and connection in caring for the elderly parent. American Journal of Family Therapy 21:27–39, 1993

7

SPECIAL APPLICATIONS

Since a couple or a family is already a group unto themselves, it has long seemed reasonable to many therapists to put couples or families together for group therapy. In this chapter several ways of applying group approaches are described, and anecdotal reports in the literature attest to their usefulness (1, 2).

In this chapter we also briefly describe the application of relationship therapy principles to consultation with couple- and family-owned businesses. We address this topic because family-run businesses play an important, though publicly underrecognized, role in contemporary society. Today, in the United States, approximately 90% of all businesses are family owned. In fact, more than 100 of the Fortune 500 businesses are family run, and family businesses produce almost half of the gross national product. It is clear that enterprising marital and family therapy (MFT) specialists might do well to consider utilizing their treatment techniques in a crossover opportunity to function as consultants in helping to resolve entrenched or crisis-generated problems in family businesses.

■ WORKING WITH RELATIONSHIPS IN GROUPS

The benefits of bringing four or five couples or families together for group psychotherapy can be enormous. These derive, in part, from the several well-known overall advantages that come from group therapy itself: instilling hope, promoting the experience of no longer feeling alone with certain concerns, and fostering the sense of belonging that comes with membership in a group (3). In addition, because many family problems have similarities, people rapidly identify with others in the group. As a result, couples and family groups provide intensive support, as well as a sense of universality, that goes well beyond that provided by either group therapy in which heterogeneous individuals participate or relationship therapy with a single family or couple.

Learning new skills is an important component of all psychotherapy, and in many ways acquiring new skills becomes even more possible within the group format. In group therapy with individuals, the goal for each member is to explore himself or herself. Since this is private affair, although conducted in public, the internal process that takes place is rarely transparent to others. However, in marital and family group therapy, in which the goal is to improve relationships, the interpersonal process is always "on the table." This transparency provides a unique opportunity for learning, and this form of learning—watching other people do it and then doing it oneself—is particularly valuable. Since couples and families frequently enter therapy requesting help in learning how to "communicate," they have models all around them of other couples and families learning and practicing new methods.

What are the curative factors in group therapy, and how can we use knowledge of these factors to guide the way we work with relationships in a group context? Here a lively debate takes place in the field. Some believe that the group process and group dynamics, and those factors mentioned above that derive from the process—such as instilling hope, fostering a feeling of belonging, and providing a safe place for airing problems—are the curative factors that come from being in a group (4). Other therapists maintain that the group impacts the individual by providing an opportunity for reality testing, which in turn allows individuals to gain a new perspective on their own distortions (5).

Therapists who lean toward the idea that the group process and group dynamics are the most important factors will likely be less active as group leaders, permitting the group to develop its own shape and identity. On the other hand, those who believe in the importance of bringing out individual factors are likely to be more active leaders. Each type of approach has its benefits, and many therapists are able to skillfully integrate both by working with the group and by working with individuals within the group format.

In couples and family groups, group dynamics and individual issues are of equal importance, because there are multiple levels at which the participants operate: as members of the group, as part of a couple and/or family, and as individuals. Managing the complexity of these multiple factors is the task of the therapist. The therapist carries out this task by assiduously maintaining the many boundaries, using the group's notable resources (energy, ideas, affect, and experience), and actively fostering the development of cohesion. The complexity of the interactions and the energy required to organize and work in the multiple-family and couples group format sometimes make the task of this kind of therapy seem daunting to therapists. However, the return on investment is well worth the output.

Cotherapy

Cotherapy is another variable to consider, not just with couple or family groups, of course, but with conducting all relationship therapy. Some therapists and participants favor cotherapy, but many do not. The advantages are easy to see: two heads are better than one, four eyes are better than two, and with a teammate for support one may feel a little bit more adventuresome in trying out new tactics and exercises. On the other hand, conflict between therapists that may result from their having different points of view can become a problem. When such conflict arises, the therapists must resolve it so as to avoid interfering with the therapy.

In cotherapy, which to some degree reflects a close relationship between two persons, participating couples and families tend to project their beliefs, feelings, and expectations—both positive and negative— onto the therapist team. Although this phenomenon is common to therapy in general, transference becomes a very powerful force in couple and family groups, particularly when the cotherapists are actually a couple themselves. The comparison to parents is all too obvious.

There is little clinical data in the literature to support using cotherapists in couple and family groups. Despite this lack of data, the use of cotherapy is common in therapist training and in inpatient treatment settings.

Relationship Groups: Format and Organization

A number of possible formats can be used for group therapy with couples or families. Groups can be *open* with respect to membership, as in the case of drop-in groups, or *closed,* as in the case of ongoing groups in which trust, confidentiality, and intimacy are carefully cultivated. Groups can be *open-ended and ongoing,* with no anticipated closing date; *time limited,* as when meeting weekly for 8 weeks, or for a brief single, yet intense, session taking place, for example, in a day or over a weekend; or *time-limited and intensive,* as in the case of weeklong residential workshops.

Each of these formats has its place. A family or couples group held for an intensive period of time, such as an entire week, creates a different set of dynamics than does an ongoing group that meets once weekly or monthly. The ongoing group with loose membership boundaries is prevalent in inpatient settings, where the composition necessarily changes as the patient population changes. The ongoing group with relatively closed membership is more popular in the outpatient setting. The successive weekend format is a useful adjunct to outpatient treatment, particularly when it becomes difficult to convene couples or families on a regular weekly basis. The intensive group format, perhaps a week long in duration, is commonly used in residential treatment programs for substance abusers and occasionally in private practice as well.

We have developed and written about a unique model for providing group therapy to families and couples (6). For more than

20 years we have done intensive group therapy in which four or five families or couples come together in a pleasant vacation place for a week's period of time (see "Case Example" to follow). Throughout the week we eat, rest, work, and play together. The workshops are exciting and challenging, but also draining to the therapist leaders, who must orchestrate it all.

Working as a cotherapy team, we almost always include trainees—all professional therapists in their own right—as adjunct faculty. The advantages to the couples or family members of having the trainees at close hand are many: extra support, contact, fun, and professional input and energy. The theoretical base of our work in these groups is again Redecision Relationship Therapy (RRT) (see Chapter 4). In the following subsections we outline the application of group approaches in MFT in more detail.

Group Therapy With Couples

A typical couples group is made up of four or five couples, and, there are no hard-and-fast rules about who is and who is not appropriate to include in couples group therapy. However, it has been determined overall that couples groups work best with well-educated couples capable of forming good relationships. They also work best when both partners are committed to the relationship and have already had some experience with therapy. Although there are no specific contraindications to including a couple in a group, it is important to remember that emotions can run high. Group members therefore should have the capacity to tolerate anger, particularly when the anger is not directed at them.

These caveats suggest that the best approach to including a couple in a group is careful screening with respect to motivation, commitment, ego strength, and experience. Whenever possible, it is a good idea to orient each couple to the group by providing detailed information about what is likely to happen and carefully explaining the "rules" for operation—such as confidentiality, no use of alcohol or nonprescription drugs, expectations regarding attendance, payment schedules—and any other issues or guidelines the therapist considers important. This structuring is the beginning of the development of a safe environment. Also, careful outlining of the operational guidelines or rules fosters group process and the inclusion of all members.

Some special programs focusing on specific content—such as "12 Step" programs for couples, programs for abused and abusive partners, or couples therapy in which illness is a central concern—are relatively homogeneous with respect to the problem. The usual outpatient program is less homogeneous, although it does seem to work better when the couples are from more or less the same socioeconomic group and when there is not a wide disparity of ages. Having said this, it is important to note that group therapy with couples is often used when working with people with substance use disorders, major depression, and chronic illness. Couples group therapy can also be a valuable adjunct to treating couples when one of the partners has a serious medical condition such as breast cancer (7).

The goal of couple therapy, whatever the format, is to improve the quality of the relationship. When the couple is open to new perspectives, can be honest about feelings, and is ready for and capable of change, many strategies may accomplish this end. But all strategies seem to come down to one bottom line: cultivating a new type of relationship that involves interdependence. *Interdependence* is defined as a collaborative interfacing of separate, autonomous persons. Relationship therapy, then, aims to help the couple develop in a way that two separate and autonomous individuals can rely on each other but are also able to fall back on their own strengths when and if the need arises.

Typically, when a couple starts therapy, they are relationally dependent, operating with either a passive or a hostile style. The goal of the couples group therapist is to help the group develop and utilize the group's resources so that each couple, in turn, can use the group and its members as a reference point to move toward interdependence. Therapists use different means to achieve this goal. For example, early in the life of the group, structured exercises and educational material such as videos or topics for discussion are presented, setting the tone by defining what will be talked about. Once the group has formed and some degree of cohesion is evident, the group itself is used as a cotherapist. The "life cycle" of the group becomes predictable, mirroring the development of the couples and individuals from dependence to independence.

The detailed operations within the group resemble those we described for the sequence of guidelines in relationship therapy (see Chapters 3 and 4): contact, evaluation, contract, and intervention into the system, to be followed by individual work, when appropriate, and ending with some approach to creating a new and healthy system. All of these operations are enhanced and supported in a well-functioning group utilizing RRT.

Case Example

Tom (age 38 years), an engineer, and Laura (age 35), an accountant, had been married for 6 years and had a 3-year-old daughter. They first entered couple therapy because both were concerned that they were "continuously at war." Tom and Laura could not seem to have a simple conversation without at least one of them exploding—a pattern confirmed in their first two sessions. We recommended a couples group in the hope that they might gain some separation from each other by participating in the work of other couples. Although hesitant, they agreed because they found the proposal reasonable.

Tom and Laura entered the group as the fifth couple, at its beginning. It was a time-limited group of 12 weeks; each session was 2½ hours long. This group quickly formed a cohesive unit. The participants were all about the same age and in similar stages of life, and each individual was committed to making things better with their partner and to helping each other participate in the various experiences of life.

The first session was primarily a warm-up with introductions, group exercises to promote interaction, outlining of couple and individual strengths, and a first brief look at how each couple experienced their difficulty. The rules of operation for the group were reiterated and discussed.

At the opening of the second session, we structured an exercise in which each individual was asked to draw a diagram of his or her own couple relationship. Group members were next instructed to form three small groups with persons other than their partners. The task of the small group was simply for each person to discuss his or her drawings with the others. This type of activity promotes group interaction and develops a focus on the individual as well as the couple relationship.

In reporting back to the whole group on the small-group experiences, one member of Tom's group commented on the exquisite detail in Tom's drawing. On hearing this, Laura piped up: "That's him, all right. He drives me crazy! . . . He picks at every detail as if everything is connected to him. He never gets what I mean or understands me." With that statement, the work for them as a couple began.

During the fifth session Laura began to talk about being afraid of Tom, "because it's never as if he sees me or anything about me." We used this as an entrance to explore her fear in the context of her family of origin. Laura's mother had been a shy and fearful woman who had been overwhelmed by her father; Laura noted that "I must have learned it from her. I loved her so much and I always wanted to protect her, but I never wanted to be like her."

The sixth session was actually two sessions run simultaneously: a men's group and a women's group. Laura used the safety of the women's group to further explore her fears about being overwhelmed and wiped out by Tom just like her mother had been by Laura's father. Tom came away from the men's group with a new insight: that his overdetailing was a form of avoiding closeness, dating back to his childhood and relating to his relationship with his mother. He realized that avoiding closeness was something he no longer needed to do. He also came up with some ideas about how to stay in the present with Laura.

Having clarified the systemic and individual factors that resulted in their difficulties, accepted the archaic component of their individual contributions to the difficulties, and made the relevant redecisions about staying in the present, Laura and Tom could now focus on practicing the art of intimate communication for the balance of the meetings. It had become very clear during their work that their being continuously at war served the purpose of masking their individual fears of closeness. Both mistrusted their ability to remain as individuals while being in the relationship, and the group supported their new identification as strong and sufficient individuals.

In this group, managing the boundaries took the form of establishing group norms, recognizing the primacy of the couple by referring events and emotions back to the couple, and clarifying individual issues and how they related to the couple and the group. We used the resources of the group by formulating group exercises and using the exercises to trigger the relationship and individual work of each couple.

In conclusion, couples groups share some similarity with groups of individuals, yet they are different in many aspects. There are additional boundaries to manage and additional problems to solve—concrete and interpersonal as well as intrapsychic. Also, couples tend naturally to turn toward each other under stress, as if to say, "It's us against the world." These difficulties are counterbalanced by the richness of resources available to the couples group therapist, the diffusion of the intense transferences (in the form of projective identification) that develop in couple therapy, and the freedom to work with a couple as the situation dictates—either for a brief moment or through an entire session.

Group Therapy With Families

Working with families in group settings is considerably more complicated than working with any other group, whether it is a group of heterogeneous individuals or a group of couples. This complexity comes from the combination of family, individual, and group dynamics in the context of the many therapy-format options that are available. A multiple-family group therapist has to work with all of these dynamics—the group dynamics common to most groups, the familial dynamics, and the individual dynamics—and consider all formats. In addition, gender dynamics emerge as people begin to identify with same-sex group participants. Also, similar types of intra- and interfamilial generational dynamics go on as parents, adolescents, and younger children create their own subgroups.

The multiple-family group is an extremely powerful and positive experience for participants. It reduces the social isolation experienced by families, particularly troubled families; diffuses interpersonal conflicts, thus decreasing or even ending the alienation of individual family members; and serves as a vehicle to enhance communication, promote individuation, and support a positive sense of self (6).

Compared with couples group therapy, there are fewer restrictions and fewer caveats to guide the therapist when deciding whom to include in multiple-family group therapy (MFGT), since the presence of children changes everything. It is not always possible even to begin to guess which children will act up or act out, who will actively participate and who will not, and how parents will react to the children—their own and other people's. These variable factors are actually the meat of MFGT. More often than not, the behavior of the children and the parental response to that behavior constitute the key to the intrafamilial dynamics—the system.

Because children are involved, it is more difficult to prepare families for group therapy. It is essential to provide parents with enough information about what will happen so that they can let each of their children know what to expect from the experience. The way parents do or do not prepare the children also becomes part of the observational data about that family's system.

It is also important to structure the group population in such a way that children can form one or more peer groups. For instance, a single teenager assigned to a group of predominately latency-age children will feel isolated. It is also important to compose groups along structural dimensions. For instance, including a single mother in a group in which the other parents are in couples sometimes creates problems of misunderstanding and loneliness, among others.

Marital and family group therapy is an important component of treatment with many of the special population groups (as discussed in Chapter 6). When the subject of the group is parent training, it is very helpful for the entire family to be available to practice negotiation skills and boundary management. When a family member has a chronic illness, MFGT provides an invaluable resource for education, support, catharsis, and refocusing of energy away from the disabled person and toward the family in its efforts to move forward. When substance abuse is the issue, MFGT provides the combination of confrontation and support that moves the using person into the appropriate treatment program. In addition, MFGT is the treatment format of choice for families participating in a residential program. MFGT is cost-effective and often serves as a vehicle for providing relationship therapy in community counseling centers and public mental health facilities that serve a number of low-income families who otherwise would not receive treatment.

Several elements are important in leading multiple-family groups. As in all groups, two of the therapist's important roles are *managing boundaries* and *providing safety*. Failure to adequately manage boundaries results in anxiety. Because of the way children learn, it is not enough in MFGT simply to state the rules and guidelines that provide safety. In family groups it is essential to *model* the rules by encouraging people to speak their mind and by being alert to the individual family's responses when the group norms are different from its own. In MFGT, safety is crucial above all else and is provided when the therapist is active in structuring the group's activities.

Another key element in successful MFGT is *formulating developmentally appropriate contact with each member of the group apart from their roles in their families and in the whole group.* A talking group excludes young children when they are present, and this gives them the wrong message about the purpose of family. An exclusively play-oriented group, on the other hand, excludes the parents, unless it is really being conducted as a parental learning experience. Fortunately, when five or six families come together with two therapists (and perhaps some trainees as well), several group activities can go on simultaneously, with the activity groups forming readily because of the large number of available people.

Therapy in the context of MFGT is an active process. The therapist has multiple tasks, some of which are

- To make contact both with individuals and with families as a unit
- To develop interactions that help families reveal their stories
- To devise exercises that promote group cohesiveness
- To encourage interaction and movement
- To provide the requisite educational or stimulus material, if required by the context

As participants see other families and persons at work, they very quickly become confident that they too can consider and work on their own problems productively. Group members as friends and equals support and confront one another, and, when appropriate, they cheer other participants on. After listening, they comment on similarities in life situations, as well as point out discrepancies and incongruities that are obvious to them but probably escaped the speaker's notice.

This group interaction is often more valuable overall than any comment or direction from the therapist, because group members frequently invest the group leaders with the cloaks of their parents or other influential authority figures from the past and, therefore, react to them by either adapting or rebelling. As they do this, the opinions and judgments of other group members assume greater importance.

Group members work on their own problems in private while watching someone else working on similar issues. Although seemingly inactive at the moment, they use the work that the active member is doing to stimulate new thoughts on their own difficulties.

By frequently dividing the large group into smaller units, the therapist can utilize the resources of all the possible subgroups—such as men's, women's, parents', and kids' groups—and this allows individuals to explore different role identifications and to examine their relationships from other perspectives.

In MFGT it is very important for the therapist to focus on people's strengths. In troubled families, people are forever giving out negative and critical messages both to each other and to others in the world around them. Families with problems have often lost sight of their strengths as a total unit and as individuals, so that whenever a therapist can use a strength as a starting point, both the family and the group begin to flourish.

Since multiple-family groups are complex and dynamic life forms, it is impossible to depict the group experience through a specific example of one family's participation. Therefore, we will simply outline the activities of one intensive MFGT.

As background explanation, we should say that for more than a quarter of a century, we have been experimenting with the various formats for both couples group therapy and MFGT. We continue to like the residential, intensive workshops because they work best. They are also quick, complete, and actually fun. By the time participants arrive at the workshop setting, they have already overcome much of their initial resistance; those who have not quickly prepare themselves for change as they begin experiencing the group in operation.

By creating a complete, protected environment in the intensive workshops, we can observe couples and families in detail. We can watch how people interact at meals and how they talk to each other outside the therapy room. We listen to who tells whom where to sit. We watch who cuts the children's food, and we notice who responds when the milk is spilled, and how. Between the sessions, couples and families come and go as they choose. Playing with them as well as working, we get to know them in widely different settings.

Case Example

This particular group was a six-day residential group with five families, two therapists (ourselves), and five trainees. Three families came from our practice, and two had been referred by other therapists who knew of our work. In all, there were 22 participants: three two-parent families and two single-parent families, with the number of children as few as one to as many as six. The children ranged in age from 8 to 16, with a clear latency-age group and a somewhat smaller adolescent group. (See Table 7–1 for a brief look at the structure and organization of a typical week.)

Multiple-family group therapy can be a powerful experience, either by itself or as an adjunct to other forms of therapy. It makes use of the resources available to large groups and requires ingenuity and activity by the therapists. An interesting finding from our long history of conducting MFGT supports the relevance of the systems concept: It is not necessary for everyone in a family to make significant individual changes; the family will experience enduring change even when only one individual changes.

Network Therapy

Network therapy is a form of family group intervention that extends the pool of resources from the individual through the couple and the family to a larger social context.

In some situations individuals are so firmly entrenched in a given life position that their immersion within a serious problem situation impacts the rest of the family. In such a circumstance it may be useful to convene a special "network" of concerned people and then enlist its members in helping both the individual and the family.

TABLE 7–1. **Redecision Relationship Therapy: Multiple-family group format**

Day		Group type	Events
One	Evening	All families together	Introductions
			Discussion of rules and guidelines for the week
			Large-group exercises to set positive tone
Two	Morning	All families together	Discussion of goals
		One family at a time	Acquiring information about system
			Contract formation
			Homework for lunch break
	Afternoon	Separate parents and kids groups	Couple and family issues in parents groups
			Exploration of individual and family issues, and formation of supportive alliances in kids group
Three	Morning	Two family groups— three families in one group, two in the other	Systems interventions
	Afternoon	Men's and women's groups	Work on individual and family issues from a different perspective
Four	Morning	All families together	Large-group support and confrontation efforts for change
	Afternoon	Breaktime	Families encouraged to play and relax
Five	Morning	Large group	Check-in
		Parents and kids groups	Work on individual and couple issues

(continued)

TABLE 7–1.   **Redecision Relationship Therapy:**
              Multiple-family group format *(continued)*

Day		Group type	Events
Five	Afternoon	Families in two groups	Continuation of work on individual issues
		Men's and women's groups	Work on family system and individual issues
			Completion of contracts for change
Six	Morning	Large group—one family at a time	Summing up
			Planning for the future
	Afternoon	Large group	Termination of therapy work and good byes

Convening the network first involves having the patient or family identify suitable members. This is usually an enlightening process for people who feel isolated and alienated. The network can consist of immediate and extended family, employers, teachers and school counselors (current or former), healthcare practitioners, clergy, and friends. It next involves detailing the nature of the problem and then developing the attendees into a working group and brainstorming possible solutions.

Originally this approach was applied in situations in which a deeply troubled young person—usually one overwhelmed by the negative symptoms of schizophrenia—was unable to manage. More recently, it has been modified as part of an "intervention" for people with substance abuse problems and in situations in which a confrontational stance is indicated (8).

Family and network members are encouraged to use their resources on behalf of the index patient or family. They might decide to form a suicide watch or to act as a support group. They may be highly confrontational in helping to make necessary changes, or proactive in getting the best resources needed, such as an inpatient treatment program. Questions of confidentiality must be addressed in an ecosystemic approach and are not insurmountable. The advantages of such an approach can sometimes be tremendous.

An intervention through the network of a family or individual uses the principles and techniques of group therapy described earlier in this chapter, but it is rarely the sole intervention. For the most part it serves as the beginning of therapy.

■ CONSULTATION TO FAMILY-OWNED BUSINESSES

Working as a relationship consultant with family-owned businesses is a rewarding, exciting, and very challenging experience.

Some years ago, one of the more frequent complaints bringing a couple into therapy was a problem in their sexual relationship. Or if the couple entered treatment in the context of family therapy, at some point the marital relationship would be addressed and sexual difficulties would surface at that time as "the issue." In recent years, however, we began noticing that adults in families wanted to talk more about the family business. Perhaps this shift simply reflects a societal shift away from giving so much attention to sexual matters, with the result that more attention is being focused on business.

Or perhaps there is a significant actual, as compared with perceived, reason for this shift: more family members are in business with other family members than ever before. As we mentioned earlier, as many as 90% of the businesses in the United States are now family owned or family controlled. More people are leaving the corporate environment to start their own business, and more couples are managing their own life transitions by starting a new business.

Whatever their motivations, many people coming into relationship therapy clearly want to use their business relationship as a context for their talks. In addition, family business owners are beginning to recognize that their business problems are as much interpersonal, and particularly intrafamilial, as they are strictly business related. These same business owners also recognize, with increasing frequency, that a family therapist, schooled in the ideas of family systems, may be the best person to help them. Thus, consulting to family-owned businesses is another special application of MFT (9).

Working with family-owned businesses presents a special challenge. Because so many of the elements of working with family businesses (we include couple-owned businesses here, too) are similar to those of working with relationships in the therapeutic context, it is easy to fall into the trap of thinking that the work is actually similar. It is not. Relationships within a family business are extremely complex. The past, present, and future, ownership and management, and family dynamics all intersect. Histories between individuals predate any business relationship. People's views differ depending on age, generation, and the culture of upbringing. Personal relationships continue regardless of the business, and loyalty bonds operate independent of business ties and conflicts.

As a snapshot way of understanding the field and planning an approach to help prevent or resolve problems in family enterprises, let's look momentarily at some of the immediate issues. In families, people have or take roles, and there are discernible boundaries that help to distinguish these roles. In family-owned or -controlled businesses, people have multiple roles. Family members, in addition to being parents and children, siblings, or cousins, are shareholders and managers; each of these positions has its own role definition, responsibilities, and attitudes (10).

For instance, consider Jeffrey Carson. The founder and majority owner of a prosperous plumbing-supply business, he is the leading shareholder as well as the CEO. He wears four hats: parent, spouse, CEO, and shareholder. He has three children, and the oldest son, a business school graduate, works as the accountant and treasurer. The oldest is paid partly in stock and is a small shareholder, whereas his younger brother, who works part-time in the shipping department, is not. An uncle who loaned Jeffrey money to get started is a shareholder, but he does not work in the business. A hard-working senior manager is neither a family member nor a shareholder.

Each person, in each role, has a different interest, and some have several interests. Shareholders want a return on their investment, which means taking money out of the company. Managers want the business to do well so that their jobs will be secure, a goal that often means plowing profits back into the company. Most family members, on the other hand, are usually more interested in the quality of relationships and the future than in present security and immediate profits. Some family members, of course, are interested only in the immediate cash and perks of the family business.

It is essential to understand the play of forces that are unique to family businesses as compared with families. As another example: In a family board meeting a heated exchange between a business owner and his employee son occurred, and the CEO fired his son. The son reflexively said, "You can't fire me, I'm your son!" thereby outlining the role conflict. The family therapist (who was not the consultant), honoring the generational boundary, had previously suggested that the father step aside and let his son take over. This was not acceptable to the father. Although he loved his son, he did not believe he was ready yet to run the large, successful business.

We have found that the three-stage model is a useful way to approach the unique interfaces and complexities encountered when consulting to family businesses. The process of consulting to family-owned businesses is summarized in Table 7–2.

In Stage I of the initial consultation period, it is essential to make contact with each of the key players and to evaluate carefully the influence of behind-the-scenes family members such as spouses and grandparents. We pointed out earlier that it is possible to see enduring change in the family even when only one person has changed. This is much less likely to happen with family-owned businesses, or any business for that matter, unless that "one person" happens to be the key person in the business.

A contract that recognizes the role of interpersonal factors is also essential. For instance, it is important to clarify how improving the relationship between two brothers will benefit the business before tackling the repair of that relationship. The contract will be even more effective if it recognizes specific systemic effects, such as how the parents, by stepping in to help their children, in fact interfered with their working together successfully. It would be further valuable to include some suggestion of how the sibling conflict actually helped the parents, who had retired some years earlier. The perpetual conflict kept them involved in the family business, to continue to give purpose and meaning to their life.

The individual or intrapersonal work of Stage II takes on a different character when the consultation model is followed. The therapist acts as a coach or mentor to the individuals in their search for information about themselves. One frequently used method of data gathering in the consultation mode is the genogram (see Chapter 2). The genogram helps identify transgenerational themes while allowing the participants to maintain a relatively safe emotional distance.

TABLE 7–2. **Stages in family-business consultation**

Stage	Goal	Tasks
Stage I	Reorient priorities	Define family and business systems
		Identify key people and processes
		Form contracts
		Intervene to challenge the conventional mind-set, myths, beliefs, and values
Stage II	Rethink individual alternatives	Identify barriers to the change process
		Educate about the benefits of change
Stage III	Accept and implement new vision	Coach to develop confidence and competence
		Develop new team perspective and interactions

The work of this, the second, stage—again remembering it is being conducted in the consultation mode—is always carried out by staying in the present and keeping current cognitive abilities intact. Regression is not helpful.

In Stage III, reintegration, strategic planning is applied to family relationships. *Strategic planning* is a term and a function that family business members already know and feel safe with, and it is future oriented.

It is also important to recognize that time has a different meaning for consultation in business than it does for therapy. In therapy we typically meet weekly in the early phase and space visits out as therapy progresses. In the consultation model we might meet for a day or weekend and then not again for 1 to 2 months. A lot can happen in an interval between sessions, so the family business consultant plans for that interval by assigning tasks, conducting experiments, keeping in phone contact, meeting with subgroups or individuals, and otherwise keeping the process alive.

In summary, working as a consultant is a similar and yet very different process than working as a therapist. The boundary between consultation and therapy must always be clear from the start and needs to be very carefully established and followed. The consultant relationship is also different from the therapist-patient relationship. The consultant usually becomes more personally involved in the problem-solving process than the therapist does. A coach-mentor is more of a friend than a therapist, and the consultant is more of an employee than the therapist is. Each of these factors affects the interchange between the family business members and the consultant and at times may prove difficult for the therapist/consultant to manage.

Nevertheless, working as a relationship consultant with family-owned or -controlled businesses is a professionally stimulating and challenging experience. We are called on and can use all that we know about individuals, about systems, and about being an excellent therapist. All apply.

■ REFERENCES

1. Donovan J: Short-term couples group psychotherapy: a tale of four fights. Psychotherapy 32:608–617, 1995
2. Kaslow N, Suarez A: Treating couples in group therapy. Family Therapy Collections 25:3–14,1988
3. Yalom I: The Theory and Practice of Group Psychotherapy, 4th Edition. New York, Basic Books, 1995
4. Scheidlinger S: Group dynamics and group psychotherapy revisited: four decades later. Int J Group Psychother 47:141–160, 1997
5. Munich R: Group dynamics, in Comprehensive Group Psychotherapy. Edited by Kapan HI, Saddock BJ. Baltimore, MD, Williams & Wilkins, 1993, pp 21–32
6. McClendon R, Kadis L: Chocolate Pudding and Other Approaches to Intensive Multiple Family Therapy. Palo Alto, CA, Science & Behavior Books, 1983
7. Carter C, Carter R: Some observations on individual and marital therapy with breast cancer patients and spouses. Journal of Psychosocial Oncology 12:65–81, 1994
8. Speck R, Attneave C: Network therapy, in Changing Families, Edited by Haley J. New York, Grune & Stratton, 1971, pp 312–332
9. McClendon R, Kadis LB: Family therapists and family business: a view of the future. Contemporary Family Therapy 13:641–651, 1991
10. Kadis LB, McClendon R: A relationship perspective on the couple owned business. Family Business Review 4:413–424, 1991

8

ETHICAL CONSIDERATIONS

There's a story of a wise man who was asked to mediate a dispute between two people. He listened to the first person and responded, "You are right." After listening to the second person, he also responded, "You are right." A puzzled bystander asked the wise man, "How can they both be right?" The wise man responded, "You are right, too."

Ethical dilemmas in relationship therapy are like this story. It is much easier to pose the questions than to resolve them, and there are many answers to what is "right." In keeping with this irony, we don't try to provide any answers in this, our last, chapter. For the most part, there is no single answer to the ethical questions raised in the situations specific to working with relationship units. It is, however, important to think about and openly discuss these issues; they are ever-present, and we have a commitment to deal with, rather than avoid, reality. We serve as models for confronting difficult issues, and failure to discuss ethical issues could leave us vulnerable to our own prejudices.

Numerous ethical decisions arise in treatment situations in the course of therapy: management of the transference and counter-transference, financial accommodations, interprofessional relationships, therapist-patient boundaries, to name just a few. We will not discuss them in this chapter because they are not specific to working with relationships. Common to all therapy, these issues have been, and will continue to be, discussed in the literature—and whenever therapists congregate.

Our task is to focus on those ethical conundrums that result from the dilemmas that arise in relationship therapy, because more than one person from the same family—and sometimes the entire family—is a patient at the same time. There's an additional twist: Sometimes in the context of marital and family therapy (MFT) it is discovered that an individual is being abused or neglected but cannot fend for himself or herself—such as is the case with an abused child and, in most instances, an abused woman or frail elderly person—and the therapist is mandated by law to report the perpetrator to the authorities, even if the perpetrator is a family member.

Ethical dilemmas are, as we have said, an intrinsic part of the dynamic when working with relationships. In MFT, ethical issues occur primarily in four basic contexts (1):

- Who, exactly, is the patient?
- What do we mean by confidentiality?
- How can we maintain neutrality?
- How do we deal with the increasingly imposed legal requirements?

Let's consider briefly these four questions with an eye toward helping the relationship therapist determine what is ethical behavior in any given situation.

■ DETERMINING WHO IS THE PATIENT

The overriding question for all relationship therapists is, who is the patient? In fact, in a recent analysis of ethical standards for marriage and family therapists, the responsibility to patients is described in somewhat contradictory terms (2). It is not always possible to advance the welfare of families and at the same time respect the rights of each of the persons seeking assistance within the relationship.

Balancing Individual and Family Perspectives

Cohesiveness—the sense of belonging to the same unit, of being "on the same wavelength" as your partner, of sharing the same values—is the recurrent theme in evaluating high-functioning couples and families. Cohesiveness, part of the experience of intimacy, has been shown time and again to result in more satisfaction with the relationship and better outcomes. However, the need for cohesiveness sometimes conflicts with the needs of the individual.

This paradox creates a predicament for the therapist. Which is more important: the relationship or the individuals within it? A good example of this quandary is experienced with the divorcing couple or family. One member of the couple may want the divorce, but the other does not. The person who wants the divorce might be satisfied with the outcome of treatment, whereas the other person may feel betrayed or even harmed (3).

This issue is particularly relevant when minor children are involved. For example, statistics indicate that divorce generally causes economic and social hardship to the custodial parent (usually the mother), and consequently educational and other opportunities for the children are generally decreased. Knowing this statistically significant outcome, what obligations does the relationship therapist have to the family unit that he or she is treating?

If the relationship therapist believes the family is the patient, and also has a personal belief in the institution or the sanctity of marriage, then he or she might opt for helping the marriage continue, no matter what, even if the effort to preserve the marriage might come at the cost of the development of one or both of the partners' individual autonomy. On the other hand, if the therapist personally believes in and advocates autonomy, one or both partners may grow at the expense of the marital bond and at the expense of their children's future emotional health and educational opportunities. When does the therapist help facilitate an amicable divorce, or at least a divorce in which the two sides are able to preserve rational communication and mutual consideration? This is a question of great concern particularly when the parting partners share the responsibility for raising children.

Factoring a Family's Values

Another area of ethical concern is related to the need to take into account the sociocultural perspective. Each culture has its own set of values, expectations, and rules. If we, as relationship therapists, attempt to impose our own values, the family will likely reject them—and us as well.

Therapists must always be sensitive to both the values of a family's ethnic or national culture and the problems patient families have in balancing these within the American way of life. The well-entrenched American ideal of "rugged individualism" promotes individual achievement, sometimes at the expense of the family. Families will make financial sacrifices and make emotional adjustments in the full knowledge and expectation that their children will leave home literally as well as figuratively.

Consider contrasts with other traditional family systems tied to particular cultures. For example, families of Japanese origin may support their children, especially in advanced-education endeavors, but they also expect them to stay under the family's influence throughout their lives. Families of Chinese origin depend primarily on the oldest son. He is expected to care for his parents when they become elderly, and, almost more important, he is held responsible for burying and then perpetually honoring his parents' remains.

We could expand this idea further to many other cultural, ethnic, and religious groups residing in America and also to issues related to gender. For example, many families in America are still culturally organized around the paramount needs of the adults, primarily the male adults, often to the disregard of both women and children, whose special emotional, educational, and health needs may go unperceived or may not be fulfilled.

We experience discrepancies even within the same culture. In the United States the normative value is the needs of the child; yet our actions as parents, as we have shown throughout this book, may conflict with these beliefs.

Balancing Different Value Systems

In providing relationship treatment we must work to reconcile multiple value systems: the patient family's, the therapist's, and that of the dominant society's culture (including different subcultures). When helping families, the relationship therapist walks a thin line between culturally or religiously based scripts and personal values. Moreover, it is clear that children are inevitably exposed to numerous outside influences, including peers from other family types and the entertainment media. Books, movies, and television often influence children in deciding on their goals and direction in life, which may be incomprehensible to their parents. This complexity, confusion, and possible conflict in value systems often present ethical dilemmas for the family therapist.

Part of the answer to the question of who is the patient in relationship therapy has more to do with our personal values and training than it does with the situation itself. Although the central focus of the systems therapist is the couple or the family, the contemporary family therapist is also concerned about balancing the individual's needs with those of the system. For the individually oriented therapist, the converse is true: the main focus is the well-being of the individual, and the therapist may or may not be attuned to the needs of the larger system.

But what do you do when a couple divorces after a long course of marital therapy and both partners want to continue in individual therapy with you? How should you respond when you are meeting with a family and the husband's individual therapist calls to tell you about his patient's plan to leave the marriage but that the patient is unwilling to disclose this intention in the family meetings? Or, how will you handle being called in to testify in a custody battle on behalf of one of the parents you have seen conjointly or as part of a family? These are common difficulties related to the issue of where loyalty as a relationship therapist lies. And there are no simple answers.

Making Ethical Decisions

Even the process of therapy holds potential pitfalls about which the family therapist must make ethical decisions. Typically, when reluctant members are encouraged to participate, their presence during sessions may be helpful to the family but not necessarily to the individual, who would choose, given the chance, not to be there at all. The same predicament is true when people are encouraged to express their angry feelings—doing so might prove hurtful to other people, even though it may help the person who is ventilating—or when people are encouraged to broadcast information, maybe about a medical difficulty or even a medication they are taking, and this information causes shame, pain, and harm in the present.

Finally, more and more families are facing the problem of what to do with a chronically ill or mentally incapacitated member of the family. The question is whether to use resources for in-home care or to encourage institutional or other out-of-home care. Each of these questions presents problems. So again the relationship therapist is faced with the question of who is the patient—a decision made that much more problematic when it is not possible for everyone, or even anyone, to come out a winner.

■ CONFIDENTIALITY AND PRIVACY

Although confidentiality is the bread and butter of psychotherapists, maintaining confidentiality can get complicated in multiperson groups such as couples or families. Concerns about family secrets, privileged communication, and rights to privacy are all parts of confidentiality. But when the patient is the family, everyone in the family may have different views of what confidentiality means. A privileged communication can quickly become a secret, and someone's right to privacy may collide with another person's belief in openness and the right to know.

Family secrets lead to the development of coalitions resulting in out-groups and in-groups. Such secrets clearly cause problems for the individual members of the family, for the family unit, and for the therapist, who may be the container, at least temporarily, of the secrets.

It is, however, an oversimplification to just say that family secrets are absolutely forbidden, because in some circumstances disclosure to other family members could be extremely harmful to the person and to the relationship. An obvious example of a situation in which disclosure could be hurtful includes when a family member with AIDS is reluctant to reveal the condition to an infirm elder member. Another is a circumstance in which one partner in a couple had an affair long ago; disclosing it now might needlessly cause great pain to the spouse. And finally, what about the 17-year-old girl who has not told her parents, who are devout right-to-life believers, that she has had an abortion?

The field of reproductive biology provides other examples in which the child's right to know his or her genetic heritage is at odds with the parent's right to privacy. Therapists are accustomed to dealing with the quandary of parents when deciding to tell their adopted child about the adoption and whatever is known about the birth parents. They are less familiar, however, with the contemporary variant of that issue: whether to tell children about their biological heritage when conception was the product of donated sperm or egg, or both. And how does one handle the situation with the wife and mother who will not reveal to her current husband and children that years earlier she had a baby that was given up for adoption and now she has been contacted by the grown-up child. Whenever individual choice or history affects other people, we are faced with an ethical dilemma about confidentiality. The choices can be perplexing.

Privileged communication presents a similar problem. It creates alliances between family members, and in families with problems, one person's alliance is another person's coalition. The same can be true for privileged communication between one family member and the therapist. Any communication that remains privileged creates a special relationship that can become problematic when it comes to light. The possible list of conundrums seems endless.

In individual therapy all communication is privileged. In family therapy everything is expected to be out in the open. But how does a patient develop trust unless there is the option of exploring confidences with a trusted other? Therefore, determining what is and what is not a privileged communication becomes an ethical dilemma for any therapist working with a multiperson group.

The right to privacy is another issue that relates to both who the patient is and what is to be considered confidential. Most of us take this right for granted, but in some families privacy is taken as an affront and is equivalent to keeping secrets. Yet, how do young persons begin to explore their own developing adult identities, emotionally and sexually, if they cannot keep these explorations private? Should teenagers' diaries, or even mail, be considered to be privileged communication? If so, what about the 13-year-old girl receiving letters from her 25-year-old boyfriend, who is currently in prison? Can her mother stop them from being delivered and have them deposited instead in a post office box that her daughter cannot access? That too creates a dilemma.

■ THERAPEUTIC NEUTRALITY: IS IT ALWAYS ADVISABLE?

Like confidentiality, an attitude of neutrality maintained by the therapist contributes to patients' feeling safe enough to reveal themselves openly in the therapy process even when other members of their family are present. Yet neutrality is extremely difficult to achieve in multiperson groups, in which there is a constant pull to take sides.

Neutrality is also difficult to achieve given therapists' own inherent personal biases about gender, age, ethnicity, equality, individual or group values, and divorce and remarriage. In addition, therapists have their own particular views about matters such as keeping family secrets, using interventions that may be deceptive, and advocating a certain position such as is sometimes necessary with certain parenting dilemmas.

One attempt to take various biases into account is what is often called the "multidirected partiality" approach (4). In this approach the therapist is expected to take sides with everyone whenever it seems appropriate to do so.

Ethical dilemmas about neutrality are intrinsic to couples and families; they occur in the context of life's many difficult situations. In conducting relationship therapy with highly troubled marriages or families, the therapist at some point consciously makes a choice either to stay neutral or to advocate a position. This choice is, of course, more difficult to make when the abused persons are not powerful enough, either physically, socially, or financially, to make a choice for themselves (as with economically dependent children and wives) or else are unable to make such a choice (as with the destitute, frail elderly). Yet, in our role as teachers and experts on mental health, our choice of the alternative solutions we present and the supportive resources we furnish may make the difference between a family member's, in the extreme situation, either submitting to an abusive situation or killing the abuser or, in the best of choices, exiting the relationship in the safest way, having been well prepared for this eventuality by the therapist.

As mentioned earlier, the direction of the field of relationship therapy has recently changed as a result of awareness of a growing ethical dilemma. In the face of abuse, any kind of abuse, it is widely held that the therapist must take a stand to protect those who cannot protect themselves.

■ MANAGED CARE AND OTHER THIRD-PARTY ISSUES

Many issues are engendered with regard to third parties such as managed-care organizations, insurance companies, referral sources, schools, and the law. The specifics of these issues tend to differ among localities. The requirements to report child abuse and neglect, sexual abuse, and elder abuse are clear, but the act of doing so has implications for both patients and therapists. And certainly it is hard for a client to trust a therapist who is under obligation to report incidences disclosing such acts, past or present.

Still, despite the law, it is not always clear how serious an action must be in order to report it. Hence, the therapist must decide whether or not to report, when and under what circumstances to report, and just how much information the third party should be given.

Managed care presents obstacles to traditional practice and good patient care in some areas that have already been addressed: privacy and confidentiality. Two additional problem areas arise in the context of managed care: the medicalization of therapy and the use of economic, as compared with patient care, incentives to drive the system. It is these two factors, the medicalization of psychotherapy and the use of economic disincentives, that create major headaches for the therapist.

Medicalization refers to the problem created when the insured's insurance limits benefits for psychotherapy to treatment that is "medically necessary." As we have seen, people most often request relationship therapy because they have difficulty managing some part of their lives in the face of the complexity of today's world. Many do not meet the threshold criteria for a DSM-IV Axis I diagnosis (5). As a result, therapists must either turn them away—or they will turn themselves away for lack of funds—or try to find some way to rationalize an acceptable diagnosis.

Moreover, in today's managed-care environment, diagnosis itself becomes an ethical concern, since for treatment to be approved or reimbursed it is often necessary to include a diagnosis based on DSM-IV, which is driven by categories that are defined in terms of pathology. Furthermore, much of the effort in outcome research—which ultimately determines the standard of practice—is directed toward measuring success in terms of resolution of a DSM-IV condition.

Family therapists, however, tend to favor *relational* diagnoses rather than individual diagnosis, and they also prefer diagnoses that avoid a description of pathology. Therefore, many family and couples therapists come into conflict with the insurance companies and the academics and are left feeling very uncomfortable when torn between their beliefs, their desire to help the patient, and the pragmatic need to get paid.

The same is true for the length of treatment. Often the contract with the managed care company limits treatment to a few visits. The therapist is again faced with the challenge of making the treatment fit the contract, which may not meet the family's or couple's needs. This is an especially acute problem for relationship therapy because many insurance plans will not pay for any form of relationship therapy. It is important to note that there are programs that are finding a way to provide good care in the current environment.

Relationship therapy is challenging because of the complex nature of the couple and family. Ethical considerations increase that very complexity and its challenge. As therapists, educators, mentors, and coaches, it is not necessary to have specific answers to the unanswerable questions. But an integral part of the job is to model how to deal with these difficult issues. It is important to remember that each of these specific concerns—determining who is the patient, confidentiality, neutrality, and interfaces with third parties—creates serious dilemmas to which the relationship therapist must respond in almost every session. As with most ethical dilemmas, there are no absolute answers, even when the law or insurance companies impose them.

■ REFERENCES

1. Margolin G: Ethical and legal considerations in marital and family therapy. Am Psychol 37:788–801, 1982
2. Larkin M: Morality in group and family therapies: multiperson therapies and the 1992 Ethics Code. Professional Psychology: Research and Practice 25:344–348, 1994
3. Wallerstein J, Blakeslee S: Second Chances: Men, Women and Children, a Decade After Divorce. New York, Ticknor & Fields, 1989

4. Boszormenyi-Nagy I, Spark GM: Invisible Loyalties: Reciprocity in Intergenerational Family Therapy. New York, Harper & Row, 1973
5. American Psychiatric Association: Diagnostic and Statistical Manual of Mental Disorders, 4th Edition. Washington, DC, American Psychiatric Association, 1994

9

CONCLUSION

Family life is too intimate to be preserved
by the spirit of justice. It can be sustained
by the spirit of love which goes beyond justice.

Reinhold Niebuhr

This concise guide has been about the most important relationships of peoples' lives: relationships with parents, children, and spouses and other close connections. It has been about how we, as therapists, can help our patients' relationships change, heal, and survive into the future.

Many of the different available models for relationship therapy, any of which can be used in some way to achieve excellent results, have been described in this concise guide. The model we presented in detail, Redecision Relationship Therapy (RRT), draws together into a single framework the different elements of relationship therapy—systemic, individual, and psychoeducational. This practical way to work with couples, families, and family-owned or -controlled businesses accommodates ideas from any of the different schools of marital and family therapy (MFT).

As we conclude, we are, however, aware that several very important questions remain unanswered in the field of MFT.

Although the outcome research we reported on previously is encouraging, there is a large difference between the laboratory and the clinician's office, and this difference leads to questions about the applicability of some findings. Laboratory studies were conducted most often with families in which there was a diagnosable disorder in an individual family member. This sample does not represent the real world. In everyday clinical practice, couples typically enter therapy because they are unhappy or otherwise dissatisfied with their relationship. Families are usually referred by community resources for child behavior, school problems, family violence, or other similar disruptive problems. A few families enter treatment when there is a specific disorder, and relationship therapy is used either as an adjunct to medical or individual therapy or as a way to otherwise mitigate an unhappy situation.

This dilemma of the discrepancy between the laboratory and the clinical setting leads to another set of related crucial questions. First, which form of relationship therapy is most effective in the clinical setting? At the moment, it is not clear that any single form of therapy works better than any other. But again, this depends on the data used to arrive at that conclusion. What, for example, is meant by the clinical setting (are we treating disease or mitigating the subjective experience of illness?), and how is improvement defined (are we defining it in terms of patient satisfaction or based on objective criteria)?

Second, what is the best recipe for successful relationship therapy? Insight alone does not result in significant changes, and behavioral change by itself is not durable. In a general sense, what appears to be the right mix of ingredients for successful relationship therapy is any focused approach that

1. Attends to the relationship's current reality.
2. Uses information and feelings relevant to the current *process* (not necessarily the current *situation*) as a way of accessing the intrapsychic past of the individuals in the relationship.
3. Builds a new working relationship in the present.

As the field becomes more aware of the subjective nature of patient's narratives, and the problems dictated by the distortions of memory, all confounded by the therapists' own subjectivity, it seems unlikely there will be any more definitive data for answering this recipe question (1).

An integrative approach seems to be the direction the field is taking in the 1990s as entirely new "trans-theoretical" models (2) are being developed and evaluated. In commenting on the "integrative revolution," Lebow notes that "even the broadest disjunction, that between individual and family therapy, is regularly negotiated" (3, p. 2). He goes on to point out some of the advantages of an integrated model: flexibility, acceptability to patients, and the ability to be tailored to meet individual therapist needs.

An important consideration in an integrated model is what elements of seemingly conflicting theory, strategy, or technique are to be combined and how. The RRT model, detailed in Chapter 4, addresses this issue directly by creating a scaffolding that allows elements of theory, strategy, and technique to be integrated seamlessly. It uses the past to inform, rather than to explain, the present. Patient's stories about themselves were the basis for their early decisions and are their guidelines to actions in the present.

A final unanswered question of the field is, what are the therapist variables that are most important in determining the successful outcome of relationship therapy? For example, relationship therapists wonder what is the best stance—therapeutic neutrality, multidirected partiality, or advocacy? There is no absolute answer to this question because every situation is different. It has been suggested, however, that the approaches that rely only on systems theory—and therefore on strict therapeutic neutrality—are less able to deal with situations that require a critical judgment. This issue was addressed in Chapter 8 in the discussion of ethical considerations, where it was noted that neutrality in the face of harmful behavior may worsen an abusive situation.

We also discussed the idea of the advantage of "skilled clinicians," on the one hand, and the growing use of "standardized procedures" that are manual based and can be carried out by other than skilled clinicians, on the other hand. As yet, no specific therapist variables have been found to contribute consistently to successful relationship therapy outcomes.

Since each and every relationship is unique, no single set of skills or any total theory can apply to all relationships. The different theories and modes of approaching the dilemma of relationships simply guide therapists to respond to particular cases in ways that will be both efficient and effective.

We, as therapists, have the power to help patients heal. How we choose to use that power is both a professional and a personal decision—one influenced by theoretical training and tempered by practical experience.

■ REFERENCES

1. Stone A: Where will psychoanalysis survive? Harvard Magazine, January–February 1997, pp 35–39
2. Prochaska J, DiClemente C: Stages of change in the modification of problem behaviors. Prog Behav Modif 28:183–218, 1992
3. Lebow J: The integrative revolution in couple and family therapy. Fam Process 36:1–18, 1997

Index

Page numbers printed in **boldface type** *refer to tables or figures.*